YORK NOTES

KT-447-103

'TIS PITY SHE'S A WHORE

JOHN FORD

NOTES BY JANE KINGSLEY-SMITH

 Longman

 York Press

The right of Jane Kingsley-Smith to be identified as Author
of this Work has been asserted by her in accordance
with the Copyright, Designs and Patents Act 1988

YORK PRESS
322 Old Brompton Road, London SW5 9JH

PEARSON EDUCATION LIMITED
Edinburgh Gate, Harlow,
Essex CM20 2JE, United Kingdom
Associated companies, branches and representatives throughout the world

© Librairie du Liban *Publishers* 2007

Quotations from *'Tis Pity She's a Whore* by John Ford are from the New
Mermaids edition of the play published by A & C Black (second edition,
2003, reprinted 2004, 2005)

First published 2007

10 9 8 7 6 5 4 3 2 1

ISBN 978–1–4058–6186–1

Typeset by Pantek Arts Ltd, Maidstone, Kent
Printed in China

CONTENTS

PART FIVE

PART ONE

INTRODUCTION

HOW TO STUDY A PLAY

Studying on your own requires self-discipline and a carefully thought-out work plan in order to be effective.

- Drama is a special kind of writing (the technical term is 'genre') because it needs a performance in the theatre to arrive at a full interpretation of its meaning. Try to imagine that you are a member of the audience when reading the play. Think about how it could be presented on the stage, not just about the words on the page.

- Drama is always about conflict of some sort (which may be below the surface). Identify the conflicts in the play and you will be close to identifying the large ideas or themes which bind all the parts together.

- Make careful notes on themes, character, plot and any sub-plots of the play.

- Why do you like or dislike the characters in the play? How do your feelings towards them develop and change?

- Playwrights find non-realistic ways of allowing an audience to see into the minds and motives of their characters, for example, through an aside or music. Consider how such dramatic devices are used in the play you are studying.

- Think of the playwright writing the play. Why were these particular arrangements of events, characters and speeches chosen?

- Cite exact sources for all quotations, whether from the text itself or from critical commentaries. Wherever possible find your own examples from the play to back up your opinions.

- Where appropriate, comment in detail on the language of the passage you have quoted.

- Always express your ideas in your own words.

These York Notes offer an introduction to *'Tis Pity She's a Whore* and cannot substitute for close reading of the text and the study of secondary sources.

 **CHECK THE BOOK**

Renaissance Drama ed. by A. R. Braunmuller and Michael Hattaway (Cambridge UP, 2003) is a good introduction to the genre and contains an essay on *'Tis Pity She's a Whore*.

READING *'TIS PITY SHE'S A WHORE*

'Tis Pity She's a Whore by John Ford, written in about 1631, is an unashamedly sensational play. It features an incestuous kiss between brother and sister; a visibly pregnant woman dragged across the stage by her hair; and a man, covered in blood, wielding a dagger on which a human heart is impaled. The play was written to shock its original audience and it is perhaps even more powerful today, when the part of Annabella can be played by a woman (in Ford's time the role was taken by a boy), and when we are less familiar with brutal displays of violence in the theatre (or, for that matter, the presence of real organs).

Yet whilst the play attains its most striking effects through performance, it is also provocative in terms of language, style and theme. This is why *'Tis Pity She's a Whore* merits careful reading and further study. Beyond its sensational combination of sex and violence, Ford's tragedy raises questions about conformity and transgression, and about the ways in which our emotional lives are shaped by external authorities, ideas that are still relevant to the twenty-first century.

The play's author, John Ford (1586–1639?), was a lawyer, poet and dramatist in early seventeenth-century London. From about 1628 to 1633, he wrote the plays for which he is now most famous, including three tragedies – *The Broken Heart*, *'Tis Pity She's a Whore* and *Love's Sacrifice* – and a history play, *Perkin Warbeck*. Yet despite his success, Ford may have been conscious that he was living at the end of a great theatrical era, after Christopher Marlowe, William Shakespeare and John Webster. The London stage of the 1620s and 1630s was far less original, often depending on revivals of old plays rather than offering its own innovations, and Ford reflects this condition of 'belatedness' by looking back to Shakespeare, in particular, to find inspiration: *'Tis Pity She's a Whore* rewrites *Romeo and Juliet*; *Love's Sacrifice* rewrites *Othello*.

Dominated by revenge tragedy, this earlier drama may have influenced Ford's work in other ways. A play still performed in the Caroline period (though it had been written as early as 1587) was *The Spanish Tragedy* by Thomas Kyd.

> **CONTEXT**
>
> A pig's heart was probably used in the original performance. More gruesome still, in a play called *The Battle of Alcazar* by George Peele (1598) three lots of sheep's entrails, liver, heart and lungs, were used to represent the disembowelling of three men on stage.

> **CONTEXT**
>
> 'Caroline' here means relating to the reign of Charles I (1625–49). 'Jacobean' refers to the reign of James I (1603–25).

This revenge tragedy featured a man biting out his own tongue and spitting it on to the stage. In 1591, *Tancred and Gismund* by Robert Wilmot included a woman being made a present of her dead lover's heart. She kissed it before drinking poison. Success in the theatre of the 1630s might have seemed to require the dramatist to surpass these violent spectacles or at least to seek out some other form of scandal. Incest, for example, had featured in a number of Jacobean plays, usually in a minor role. Where Ford differed from his predecessors was in focusing on incest between a brother and a sister, rather than more distant relatives, and in making these figures the tragic (and sympathetic) **protagonists** of his play. It is in this respect that Ford was perhaps most daring.

Before considering the play's treatment of incest in more detail, it is worth pausing over the notoriety surrounding its title. In 1831, an editor of Ford's works, John Murray, referred to the play as *Annabella and Giovanni*, explaining that 'This title has been substituted for a much coarser one'. In 1955, the literary critic Barrett Clark recalled how his university tutor had renamed the play *'Tis Pity She's Wanton,* in a seminar, because 'there were ladies present'. As recently as 1988, when the National Theatre sought corporate sponsorship for its production directed by Alan Ayckbourn, would-be sponsors made it a condition that the title be changed (it was not).

In the 1630s, the word 'whore' was much more commonly used than in the twenty-first century, partly because its meaning was much broader. It did not necessarily suggest prostitution or even promiscuity but could be applied to any woman who had sex outside of marriage, even only once. Thus, the term 'whore' would have seemed more fitting to describe Annabella in Ford's time than it does now.

What Ford's original audience *would* have found confusing is the title's suggestion that the play focuses on a woman's sexual transgressions rather than incest, and its urging them to pity Annabella for falling victim to lust. Possibly, Ford wanted to save the revelation of incest for the opening scene of the play, using a title provocative enough to get an audience into the theatre before unveiling his more titillating subject matter. The play allows its audience to 'forget' that the love it focuses on is incestuous for quite long periods.

 CHECK THE BOOK
Other plays featuring incest include Beaumont and Fletcher's *A King and No King* (1611) and Thomas Middleton's *Women Beware Women* (1621). The former is perhaps closest to Ford in looking at brother-sister incest, though at the end of the play it is revealed that the characters are not related after all.

More significant is the way in which the title encapsulates the moral **ambiguity** that defines *'Tis Pity She's a Whore*. Although the play is full of commentators who describe incest as a sin – against the family, against society, and against God – and whilst the plot suggests that it brings about its own punishment, Ford also encourages his audience to sympathise with the incestuous pair, even to the point of identifying with them. At times, Annabella and Giovanni appear just like Romeo and Juliet, defying their fathers and their stars, to pursue their secret love affair. It might strike us that Ford wants us 'to have our cake and eat it'. We are allowed the pleasure of sympathetic engagement with the couple but this finally gives way to moral condemnation. Nevertheless, sympathy can work to stimulate the audience's mind as well as its heart, and it is through the lovers, particularly in the early stages of their relationship, that Ford raises some interesting questions. For example, the unselfish devotion that they feel for one another, with Annabella willing to die to protect Giovanni, may strike us as more admirable than the greed and lust that motivate the other citizens of Parma. Is incest, we might ask, really worse than murder? Adultery and faithless love inspire revenge plots in the play. Even marriage negotiations lead to street brawls and the accidental death of Bergetto. Yet the Cardinal is outspoken in his condemnation of the incestuous couple, though he has no qualms about pardoning the murderous Grimaldi.

Ford's play encourages us to re-examine our moral values and to question the authority figures who represent and enforce those values. For example, the Cardinal declares ''Tis pity she's a whore' (V.6.159) shortly after seizing all the property of the dead for the use of 'the Church' (V.6.149). The Friar has more integrity, but he is also ineffectual. He cannot offer Giovanni a reason why incest is unlawful other than the fact that it is. Nor does he linger to see the ending of the tragedy, despite his apparent devotion to Giovanni and his responsibility for Annabella's marriage. Even Florio, though a generous and apparently loving father, remains in the dark, ignorant of his children's real feelings. In a world where the figures who try to impose law and who threaten punishment are either more corrupt than the play's supposed 'criminals' or seem themselves to lack the moral convictions that they preach, we might be more sympathetic to Giovanni and Annabella's decision to make their own rules and to invent their own world.

CHECK THE BOOK

In a short story by Angela Carter called ''Tis Pity She's a Whore' (*Granta* 25 [1988], 179–98), the Florio character is much more isolated from his children: 'Since his wife died, the rancher spoke rarely. He lived far out of town. He had no time for barn-raisings and church suppers.'

To conclude, one of the reasons why *'Tis Pity She's a Whore* continues to work as a play – in performance and on the page – is that it does not provide answers to the questions it provokes. Is Giovanni a heroic rebel, struggling against traditional moral values, who kills his lover in order to free them both from a corrupt world? Or is he is a dangerous sociopath who is driven by jealousy and lust to commit murder? Or is he both? The difficulty of deciding, and thence of determining the play's moral position, is part of its continued fascination – an effect that lingers long after the more gory spectacles are forgotten.

 QUESTION
You might consider how many times the word 'incest' is used in the play. What does this tell you? Do Giovanni and Annabella use it to describe their love? (Look at Act V Scene 5).

PART TWO

THE TEXT

NOTE ON THE TEXT

CONTEXT

A **quarto** is a small, cheaply-printed edition of a play, more like a pamphlet than a book. Since the play belonged to the acting company, the author did not necessarily earn any money from this publication and was not always included on the title-page.

'*Tis Pity She's a Whore* was first published in 1633 in a quarto text (Q) containing a dedication signed by Ford himself. It is assumed that Q represents an authorised version of the play, and this is the text upon which all subsequent editions are based. In 1652, Q was bound together with six other Ford quartos and published under the title *Comedies, tragi-comedies; and tragaedies*. It was not published again until 1744 when '*Tis Pity* was included in Robert Dodsley's *Select Collection of Old Plays* (revised 1780). In the twentieth century the play was regularly re-edited, including important editions by N. W. Bawcutt (1966), Brian Morris (1968), Derek Roper (1975), Marion Lomax (1995) and Simon Barker (1997). The edition used here is the New Mermaids edited by Martin Wiggins (second edition, London and New York, A & C Black, 2003, reprinted 2005).

SYNOPSIS

Giovanni, a student at the University of Bologna, has returned to Parma with his tutor, Friar Bonaventura, where he finds himself consumed by sexual desire for his sister Annabella. The Friar warns him that incest is a mortal sin and urges him to struggle against it by means of prayer and fasting.

Annabella, meanwhile, is encouraged by her father to choose a husband from among a number of potential suitors: Grimaldi, a Roman gentleman and soldier; Lord Soranzo, a rich and handsome nobleman; and Bergetto, the foolish heir to his wealthy uncle, Donado. Competition for Annabella's hand in marriage is fierce – Soranzo's servant, Vasques, gets into a fight with Grimaldi – but the only man she seems to love is her brother, Giovanni. Determined to find out why the latter is so melancholy, Annabella makes him confess that he is in love with her. She then confesses that she returns his affection. They swear an oath to be true to one another and leave the stage to consummate their union. Returning from the bedchamber, Annabella confides in her guardian, Putana, who urges her not to worry about the immorality of it – the satisfaction of desire is all that matters.

Meanwhile, the most eligible of the suitors, Soranzo, is revealed to have a far from spotless reputation. He has had an affair with a woman named Hippolita, promising to marry her if she got rid of her husband, but he has broken this vow. Hippolita, enraged, swears to take her revenge and persuades Vasques to help, promising to marry him as a reward. The situation is complicated by the fact that Hippolita's husband, Richardetto, is not really dead, but has returned to Parma with his niece, Philotis. Disguised as a doctor, he plots revenge against Soranzo for his wife's infidelity. He gives Grimaldi a poison with which to anoint his sword so that when he stabs Soranzo the blow will be fatal.

The negotiations for Annabella's marriage are moving towards a conclusion. She rejects Bergetto who subsequently falls for Philotis. He decides to marry her without his uncle's knowledge. Annabella then rejects Soranzo, though she promises that if she marries anyone it will be him. Almost immediately, Annabella falls sick and is discovered to be pregnant. Her pregnancy remains a secret between Putana, Giovanni and the Friar – the doctor, Richardetto, is kept from examining her too closely – but in order to avoid the shame to her reputation, it is agreed that she must marry Soranzo. By chance, on the same night as Soranzo and Annabella are betrothed by the Friar at his cell, Bergetto and Philotis have decided to be secretly married there also. In the dark, Grimaldi, who has been lying in wait for Soranzo, stabs Bergetto by mistake and kills him.

Donado, Florio and Richardetto go to the home of the Cardinal where Grimaldi is hiding and insist that he be given up to justice, but the Cardinal refuses and sends Grimaldi to Rome. Florio counsels patience, saying that Heaven will eventually bring about revenge.

Two days later, Annabella and Soranzo are married and their wedding celebrated with a great banquet. Part of the entertainment is a masque, performed by women dressed in white and carrying

> **CONTEXT**
>
> Wedding celebrations that turn into spectacles of death were extremely popular on the Jacobean and Caroline stage. An example that Ford might have remembered is the ending of Middleton's *Women Beware Women* (1621), where a masque to celebrate the wedding of Bianca and the Duke leaves six people dead including the bride and groom.

willow branches. One of these women reveals herself to be Hippolita. Wishing to make peace with Soranzo, she asks him to drink a toast with her but Vasques interrupts to reveal that it is all a plot to kill him. Hippolita alone has drunk the poisoned wine and she dies on stage cursing the newly-married couple. Having been powerfully impressed by these events, Richardetto decides to abandon his own revenge plot against Soranzo, believing that Heaven already has it in hand. He sends Philotis off to become a nun.

CONTEXT

The title-page of the 1633 **quarto** gives the title as *Tis Pitty Shee's a Whore* but this is not the only name under which the play has been published. Alternatives that avoid the use of the word 'whore' have included *Annabella and Giovanni* and *The Brother and Sister* (see **Reading 'Tis Pity She's a Whore**).

Subsequently, Soranzo discovers that his new bride is at an advanced stage of pregnancy, meaning that he cannot be the father of her child. He threatens to kill Annabella unless she will tell him the name of her lover but she refuses. Vasques intervenes, urging Soranzo to be patient until he has discovered the truth. He then persuades Putana to reveal all, after which he has her bound, gagged and blinded by a group of hired thugs (the *banditti*). Vasques and Soranzo proceed to plot their revenge against the incestuous couple. Soranzo will order Annabella to put on her wedding dress and appear at a feast to celebrate his birthday where he will presumably kill her. At the same feast, Vasques will set the *banditti* to kill Giovanni.

Imprisoned in her chamber, Annabella is full of guilt and repentance, and fears that Soranzo is planning a terrible revenge. She writes a letter in her own blood which she lets fall from the balcony. The Friar overhears her and agrees to deliver the letter to Giovanni but the latter refuses to believe that they are discovered and defiantly accepts the invitation to Soranzo's feast. The Friar now abandons all hope of saving Giovanni and decides to leave Parma.

On arriving at the feast, Giovanni is sent in to Annabella in her chamber. She tells him that their relationship is a sin for which she has sought Heaven's forgiveness and she warns Giovanni that Soranzo is planning to take revenge upon them both. In a shocking act of violence, Giovanni kisses Annabella and then stabs her to death.

Giovanni bursts into the birthday celebration, covered in blood and carrying a dagger with a human heart on the end. He explains to all the assembled guests that the heart belonged to his sister, Annabella, with whom he has been sexually involved for the past nine months and who became pregnant by him. When the story is confirmed, Florio falls dead on the spot. Soranzo begins to rebuke Giovanni but is stabbed by him and dies. Vasques intervenes and wounds Giovanni. At his signal, the *banditti* enter and kill Giovanni.

Surveying a stage that bears at least three dead bodies, the Cardinal demands an explanation from Vasques. The latter asserts that he did it all out of duty and shifts the blame on to Putana who encouraged incest. The Cardinal orders that she be taken outside of the city and burnt. Since Vasques has acted out of loyalty to his master and since he is a foreigner, he is merely banished. The Cardinal then seizes all the wealth and property belonging to the dead for the Church's use. Richardetto steps in at this point and reveals his true identity, offering to explain the tragedy in more detail. The characters leave the stage with the Cardinal expressing regret for Annabella's downfall, 'Of one so young, so rich in Nature's store,/ Who could not say, 'Tis pity she's a whore?' (V.6.159).

DETAILED SUMMARIES

ACT I

SCENE 1

- Giovanni reveals to his tutor, Friar Bonaventura, that he has sexual feelings for his sister, Annabella.

- The Friar counsels him to wrestle with his affections through prayer and fasting.

> **CONTEXT**
>
> Incest was defined in this period as the sexual relationship between those closely related by blood or by marriage (for example, between a brother and his sister-in-law or a man and his wife's daughter). (See **Themes: Incest**.)

Friar Bonaventura and Giovanni, respectively tutor and student at the University of Bologna, enter the stage in the middle of a debate. Their subject is incest and, more specifically, the sexual desire that Giovanni feels for his own sister, Annabella. Giovanni has been arguing that it is no sin to love a person to whom he is already bound by blood; it is mere social convention that keeps them apart. The Friar reminds him that incest is also against Heaven's laws and warns that God will punish him for his blasphemy. Giovanni doubts that there is anything he can do to alter his feelings but he agrees to follow the Friar's advice: to keep solitary, to fast and to pray for Heaven to cleanse him of desire.

COMMENTARY

With no sense yet that Giovanni will act on his incestuous desire, or that it will be reciprocated, he spends most of this scene attempting to justify incest theoretically. He poses a series of supposedly logical questions which he expects the Friar to agree with: 'Must I not do what all men else may – love?' (line 19); 'Must I not praise that beauty ...' (lines 20–1); 'Shall then, for that I am her brother born ...?' (line 36). The Friar, however, becomes more and more resistant to Giovanni's 'logic' and more disturbed by what it means. Incest is seen as an expression of Giovanni's intellectual pride. Hence, the Friar warns him that 'Wits that presumed/ On wit too much by striving how to prove/ There was no God ... Discovered first the nearest way to hell' (lines 4–7).

Ford's audience would have remembered what happened to Dr Faustus, another brilliant university student who misused his intellect and condemned himself to hell. More specifically, Giovanni's incestuous desire is blasphemous not only because it defies God's prohibition against incest but also because it makes Giovanni guilty of idolatry by placing his love for Annabella above his love for God:

> Must I not praise
> That beauty which, if framed anew, the gods
> Would make a god of if they had it there,
> And kneel to it, as I do kneel to them? (lines 20–3)

Significantly, Giovanni has stopped talking about the singular Christian God here in favour of a pagan notion of gods (plural). At the end of the scene he argues that fate will become his 'God', i.e. the power that directs him.

By the end of this first scene, it is not clear whether lust drives Giovanni to commit blasphemy, or whether his intellectual arrogance has partly inspired his desire. The Friar condemns them both. Nevertheless, Giovanni argues persuasively for a third possibility: that this is a romantic love, inspired by Annabella's beauty, and one that is natural and inevitable. He expresses a heartfelt desire for union with his beloved: 'One soul, one flesh, one love, one heart, one all' (line 34) in a language that seems to contradict the Friar's assumption that Giovanni has simply fallen prey to lust. From the start of the play, then, Ford prevents the audience from taking an entirely condemnatory view of either Giovanni's passion or of Giovanni himself.

GLOSSARY

2	school-points arguments in a university debate
	nice too precise
9	fond foolish
35	unhappy ill-fated
45	unranged without limit
62–3	take thy choice . . . win the Friar suggests that promiscuity, though it is a sin, is preferable to incest

---

SCENE 2

- Grimaldi and Vasques fight. Grimaldi promises to take revenge on Soranzo.

- Annabella and Putana discuss whom Annabella might marry.

- Giovanni confesses his feelings to Annabella who reveals that she returns his love.

- Brother and sister swear an oath to love one another or die. They go offstage to consummate the union.

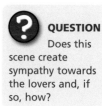

QUESTION
Does this scene create sympathy towards the lovers and, if so, how?

The scene begins with Vasques challenging Grimaldi, a professional soldier, to a fight. Grimaldi has been slandering Soranzo, Vasques' master, jealous that he is one of the suitors for Annabella's hand in marriage. Grimaldi at first disdains to engage with someone so inferior to him in rank but is forced to defend himself and looks likely to be defeated. Florio interrupts the fight and complains that they are making too much noise outside his house. He tells Soranzo that he does not need to feel threatened by Grimaldi since he has as good as secured Annabella's hand in marriage.

SCENE 2 continued

CHECK THE BOOK

Putana is clearly based on the Nurse in Shakespeare's *Romeo and Juliet* (1595).

Meanwhile, Annabella and her servant, Putana, have been watching the disturbance from a balcony. They discuss the merits of her suitors – Grimaldi, Soranzo and Bergetto – but it is the sight of an unknown man that inspires praise and admiration in Annabella. Only when Putana names him does Annabella recognise this figure as her brother, Giovanni. She wonders why he appears so melancholy. Giovanni reveals in **soliloquy** that his efforts to quench his passion for Annabella have failed and that he has decided to tell her the truth whatever it costs him.

Alone on stage together, Giovanni confesses his desire for Annabella. He offers her his dagger saying that if she does not love him then she must kill him. Annabella tells him that she reciprocates his passion and they both kneel and swear an oath to be true to one another. They kiss and leave the stage for Annabella's bedchamber.

COMMENTARY

This scene reveals the first indications of Ford's indebtedness to *Romeo and Juliet* (See **Literary background: Ford and Shakespeare**). The outburst of fighting between Vasques and Grimaldi reminds us of the fighting between Capulets and Montagues, particularly when it is rebuked by Florio as a disturbance of the peace. Similarly, the appearance of Annabella and Putana on the balcony, from whence Annabella looks down upon her lover, also recalls *Romeo and Juliet*. Like Juliet, Annabella becomes infatuated with a man before she knows his identity, but he turns out to be not the son of her enemy, as in *Romeo and Juliet*, but the son of her own father. Hence, he is even more forbidden as an object of her love.

The fact that Annabella does not at first recognise her own brother merits some further explanation. Possibly, Giovanni's melancholy makes him unrecognisable. The Friar describes how much he is altered at I.1.47–9. Annabella may also not have seen her brother for a number of years. If Giovanni were sent away to school (as was common practice with middle-class boys in the early seventeenth century) before then going on to university, Annabella would not have lived with him for any length of time since the age of seven. Ford seems to suggest that the love she feels for this stranger comes from some instinctual 'recognition' of him that could be explained as either familial or erotic.

The other important aspect of this scene is the way in which Annabella and Giovanni's expressions of mutual love mirror the marriage ceremony. Not only do they kneel and repeat the same vows but they seal the union with a kiss. Thus, although Giovanni rejects the social conventions and religious laws that condemn incest, he also invokes them indirectly through marriage in an attempt to legitimise and consecrate their love (see **Themes: Marriage**). More ominously, whilst their oath 'love me or kill me' recalls the part of the marriage ceremony in which the couple promises to stay together 'till death do us part', this equation of their love with death anticipates the violent end to which the lovers will come. Similarly, Giovanni's offer to rip up his own heart in order to prove the truth of his love **ironically** reverses the ending of the play when Annabella's heart will be displayed on stage as a symbol of their love (See **Extended commentaries: Text 1**).

> **CONTEXT**
>
> In Beaumont and Fletcher's play *A King and No King* (1611) which focuses on supposed brother–sister incest, Arbaces explains that the last time he saw his sister she was only nine years old.

> **GLOSSARY**
>
> | | |
> |---|---|
> | 1 | tackling weapons |
> | 5 | mountebank seller of medicine, famous for telling lies about their wares |
> | 9 | cast-suit person of lower rank/servant who wears cast-offs |
> | 10 | cotquean lower-class housewife |
> | 13 | prate talk |
> | 29 | ground cause of the argument |
> | 46 | wormed . . . mad dogs sometimes had a ligament under the tongue cut, in a process called 'worming', in order to prevent rabies |
> | 48 | stay your stomach satisfy your appetite, hinder your vengeance |
> | 49 | spoon-meat liquid food |
> | 54 | owing possessing |
> | 55 | Losers . . . game It is only fair to allow the loser to express his disappointment |
> | 57 | unspleened dove the dove was famous for its lack of aggression; without a spleen (believed to be a source of passion in the body) it would be particularly peaceable |
>
> continued

GLOSSARY

57	choleric	angry
80	standing upright	i.e. they cannot maintain an erection
81	crinkles . . . in the hams	bows excessively, shrinks from sex
90	wholesome	not diseased
99	draught	alcoholic drink
107	coxcomb	fool
114	shift	change
116	Spanish pavan	a slow dance
124	fool's bauble	carved stick of the professional fool (also his penis)
125	cast upon the dearth of flesh	make a decision as if there were a shortage of men (and penises)
136	partage	a share
223	bootless	pointless
259	Elysium	the pagan version of Heaven

CONTEXT

Fairs featuring puppet-shows, bear-baiting, conjurers etc. were extremely popular in early modern London. A famous example was the Bartholomew Fair held annually at Smithfield market on 24 August, and immortalised in Ben Jonson's comedy, *Bartholomew Fair* (1614). Puppet shows, often dramatising stories from the Bible or classical mythology, served to entertain and also to educate the illiterate and those with poor reading skills which may be why Donado is so derogatory about his nephew taking pleasure in them.

SCENE 3

- Florio and Donado discuss the possibility of a marriage between the latter's nephew, Bergetto, and Annabella.

- Donado insists on helping Bergetto to woo her.

Florio tells Donado that he does not need Annabella to make a match for money, but insists that she should marry for love. He and Donado agree that Bergetto should try to win Annabella's affections. Yet Donado reveals in soliloquy that he has little faith in his nephew's success. Bergetto enters, full of excitement about fairground attractions including freak-circus animals and puppet shows, and is aptly described by his uncle as a 'great baby' (line 46). His wooing of Annabella is revealed to be as inadequate as Donado had feared, requiring Donado to intervene by helping him to write her a letter.

COMMENTARY

The discussion of Annabella's potential marriage with Bergetto is given an ironic tone by the fact that at this moment she is losing her virginity to Giovanni. Yet, it also seems intended to provide some light relief after the emotional intensity of the previous scene. Bergetto is another suitor who seems quite unsuitable for Annabella – an appealing idiot, defined by his enthusiasm for childish sports. Some of the entertainments described here also had a sexual meaning, for example, 'hobby-horse' (line 51) could mean 'prostitute'. However, Bergetto's sexual inexperience, suggested later when he cannot identify the monstrous swelling that he gets when Philotis kisses him (III.5.45), implies that his pastimes are wholly innocent. His gauche attempts at flattery contrast strongly with the passionate and sophisticated praise Giovanni bestows on Annabella's beauty in the next scene.

> **CONTEXT**
>
> Ford probably borrowed Bergetto from Middleton's *Women Beware Women* which features a foolish suitor called the Ward. Both fools provide a contrast with the moral corruption and diabolic intelligence of other characters.

GLOSSARY	
7	miscarry die young
31	mint the source of the latest currency
53	Uds sa'me God save me
72	white boy favourite child
	gulled conned (out of his inheritance)
74	fit her gave her an apt answer

ACT II

SCENE 1

- Annabella and Giovanni re-enter, having had sex for the first time.
- Richardetto and Philotis are introduced to Florio's household as a doctor and his niece.

Giovanni and Annabella emerge from their bedchamber, with Giovanni asserting that the loss of virginity is a trivial thing that leaves Annabella unchanged.

CONTEXT

Although a bed features prominently on stage at the end of the play, there may have been no more than a door to suggest the presence of a bedchamber here. Perhaps the actors playing Annabella and Giovanni appeared on stage rearranging their clothes to remind the audience of their offstage antics.

The latter suggests that she would blush for shame had she not just fulfilled her 'heart's delight' (line 8). Giovanni warns that she will have to be married but Annabella insists that the idea of it is hateful to her. Giovanni makes her confirm this by swearing an oath to belong only to him.

Putana shares Annabella's joy at what has happened and urges her not to have any scruples about it – desires must be satisfied. They pretend to be busy with needlework when Florio enters and introduces Richardetto as a physician from Padua who will attend Annabella. His niece, Philotis, will play the lute and sing with her.

COMMENTARY

Once again, the love between Annabella and Giovanni is celebrated in idealised terms. For example, Giovanni describes the experience of kissing Annabella: 'Thus hung Jove on Leda's neck/ And sucked divine ambrosia from her lips' (lines 16–7). Yet there is at least one allusion to the transgressive nature of their desire. In classical mythology, this kissing was far from consensual: Jove raped Leda in the guise of a swan.

Putana's response to the couple's union may also be intended to reactivate the audience's moral judgement. Putana's name in Italian means 'whore' and she seems entirely at ease with the idea of a 'young wench' (line 44) fulfilling her sexual desires at all costs and with whoever is available: 'father, or brother, all is one' (lines 44–5). Not only does this reinforce the idea of incest as a defiance of all limits, it also suggests the destruction of the family that will be caused by incest. Giovanni and Annabella's father, Florio, will be killed by the shock (and presumably the shame) brought on by his children's actions.

We might go on to note that the couple also anticipates suffering, even at the height of their happiness. Giovanni predicts: 'I shall lose thee, sweetheart' (line 21), and his insistence that Annabella swears an oath of loyalty and his warning to her to 'keep well my heart' (line 32) foretell his possessiveness and jealousy later in the play.

GLOSSARY

6	contents delights
40	passed over travelled through
44	the fit sexual desire
47	speech of the people gossip
64	parts accomplishments

SCENE 2

- Soranzo reflects on his love for Annabella.
- Hippolita vows revenge on Soranzo for abandoning her after she had committed adultery for his sake.
- She enlists Vasques as her accomplice.

Soranzo is reading Italian love poetry and contemplating his happiness in loving Annabella, when he is rudely interrupted by Hippolita, who is dressed in mourning.

She blames Soranzo for encouraging her to commit adultery with him and of breaking his promise that once her husband was dead he would marry her. She blames herself for Richardetto's death, having encouraged him to go on a notoriously dangerous journey in the hope he might be killed. Soranzo, at first, refuses to listen to her angry accusations. He then argues that none of the promises he made to Hippolita is binding since they were all sinful. Vasques warns that this is not the way to deal with Hippolita but Soranzo ignores him and exits angrily. Alone together on stage, Hippolita tells Vasques that he is too good for such a master and promises that if he will help her in her revenge against Soranzo she will marry him. Vasques agrees.

COMMENTARY

This scene alters our perceptions of Soranzo as a suitable husband for Annabella. According to both Florio and Putana, he is the best of the suitors, combining beauty, status and wealth, and his references to contemporary love poetry suggest that he might rival Giovanni in his ability to flatter Annabella. Yet, as Hippolita

CONTEXT

Soranzo is reading the work of the Italian love poet, Jacopo Sannazaro (c. 1456–1530). Sannazaro was renowned in England as the author of a poem in praise of Venice (lines 14–5) but also for his prose romance, *Arcadia* (1502), which describes a man's frustrated love.

CONTEXT

Ford's audience would have known that a woman named Hippolita might prove both lustful and dangerous. In classical mythology, Hippolita is the name of an Amazon queen who is defeated in battle by Theseus (see the opening of Shakespeare's *A Midsummer Night's Dream*). It is also the name of the married Queen of Iolcos who took revenge on a man who refused her advances by claiming that he had tried to seduce her.

reveals, he is also an adulterer and an oath-breaker, with no qualms about encouraging murder, and his passion for Annabella may be no more lasting than his passion for Richardetto's wife.

As if registering the audience's disquiet, the apparently loyal Vasques also shows himself dissatisfied with Soranzo here: by condemning Hippolita's lust and urging her to repent her sins, Soranzo antagonises her to such an extent that she begins to plot his death. Vasques himself appears willing to betray his master for the sake of the rich reward Hippolita offers – not only wealth but the status of being her husband.

Finally, the terms in which Hippolita describes her revenge: 'On this delicious bane my thoughts shall banquet' (line 160) anticipate both the means of her revenge, namely poison, and the occasion for that act, namely the banquet to celebrate Soranzo's marriage. It seems that Ford already had the later scene in mind.

CONTEXT

Poisoning was a means of death associated with Italy at this time and it recurs in many seventeenth-century **tragedies** located there. In Webster's *The White Devil* (1612), a portrait, a Bible and a helmet are all laced with poison.

GLOSSARY	
30	foil the background or setting of a jewel that throws it into relief. Hippolita imagines herself as the forsaken lover against whose image Annabella shines more brightly
50	free honourable
56	widow in my widowhood Hippolita has lost not one but two husbands
63	unedge make blunt
75	Leghorn a town south of Parma, accessed through dangerous mountain regions
138	private secret, also with a sexual meaning
141	mole secretive animal that works underground, also blind, suggesting Hippolita's blindness to Vasques' own agenda
154	good genii guardian angels
160	bane poison

SCENE 3

- Richardetto is revealed to be the (supposedly dead) husband of Hippolita.
- He tells Philotis that he has adopted the disguise of a doctor in order to observe Hippolita.
- He offers to give Grimaldi a poison with which to kill Soranzo.

Richardetto explains to Philotis that he has adopted the guise of a doctor in order to see how his faithless wife, Hippolita, will behave now that she believes him to be dead. Philotis, however, suspects that her uncle is planning 'some strange revenge' (line 15). This conjecture is affirmed for the audience by Richardetto's subsequent encounter with Grimaldi. The soldier initially asks the doctor for a love potion that he can use on Annabella but Richardetto tells him that a more serious impediment to their union is Soranzo. He persuades Grimaldi to kill Soranzo and promises him a poison with which to anoint his sword.

COMMENTARY

Richardetto's function in the play is revealed here – he is the wronged man who returns to the scene of the crime in disguise and plots his revenge through other characters. His identity as a doctor is carefully chosen, not just because it allows him access to Florio's house where he will learn more about the relationship between Soranzo and Annabella but also because it allows him to peddle drugs, including poison. We might recall that Romeo buys poison from an apothecary in *Romeo and Juliet*. The fact that Grimaldi asks for a love-potion but is offered poison instead demonstrates how closely love and death are entwined throughout the play.

GLOSSARY		
31	Nuncio	a representative of the Pope, resident in a foreign court
40	receipts	recipes
50	speed	be successful
60	Hydra	a many-headed monster from classical mythology

 CHECK THE BOOK

This notion of poisoning the blade of a sword may have come to Ford via *Hamlet* (c.1600) in which a fencing-match with poisoned foils results in the deaths of both Hamlet and Laertes.

CONTEXT

Doctors were often figures of suspicion in early modern England, their drugs as likely to kill you as to cure you. The sinister Doctor Julio in Webster's play, *The White Devil*, is so adept in the art of poisoning that he can apparently poison a fart (II.1.301–2)!

SCENE 4

- Bergetto produces a letter which he has written to Annabella.
- Donado disapproves of Bergetto's effort. He has written another one on Bergetto's behalf.

True to his promise at the end of Act I Scene 3, Donado has written a letter on Bergetto's behalf in an attempt to woo Annabella, fearing that any courtship face-to-face between them will prove disastrous. Bergetto confirms his uncle's fears by reading a letter of his own composition in which he declares that any flattery of Annabella would be a lie and that he will marry her whether she likes it or not. Donado insists that Bergetto stay indoors whilst he delivers his own letter but Bergetto makes plans to escape to the fair.

COMMENTARY

Bergetto's love letter contrasts with the fulsome praise offered to Annabella by both Giovanni and Soranzo. His comic inability to flatter and his innocent delight in puppet shows also highlight the more sophisticated and dangerous desires of these other suitors and bring some light relief to the play.

GLOSSARY		
23	**board**	make sexual advances
25	**in spite of your teeth**	whether you like it or not
41	**apish**	foolish
	motions	puppet shows

SCENE 5

- Giovanni confesses to the Friar about his relationship with Annabella.
- The Friar warns him that he is risking eternal damnation.

CHECK THE BOOK

Bergetto's insistence that he will take Annabella 'in spite of [her] teeth' recalls Middleton's *Women Beware Women* in which the Ward is particularly concerned to inspect his potential bride, Isabella's, teeth (III.3.73–4). Considering the state of dentistry at this time, his requirement that she have none missing and none that are black may be asking too much.

The Friar responds to Giovanni's revelations about the state of his relationship with Annabella with dire warnings: Heaven will be revenged upon him for his sins. Yet Giovanni seems unmoved by his threats, arguing that it is virtuous to love Annabella and praising her beauty. The Friar urges Giovanni to repent but gradually shifts his focus to the possibility of saving Annabella, suggesting first that she should be married and then that she should confess to him and be granted absolution. Giovanni agrees that the Friar may visit her but insists that she will remain true to her love for him.

COMMENTARY

This scene repeats the play's opening, except that now the relationship has been sexually consummated so the danger to the lovers' souls is even greater. The Friar and Giovanni reaffirm their earlier arguments of Act I Scene 1, suggesting the futility of a dialogue in which neither can change the other's mind. In this scene, they also disagree on the question of Annabella's marriage. The Friar urges it, perhaps in order to redirect her sexual desires into more 'lawful' channels, but Giovanni rejects the idea, insisting that it would 'damn' (line 41) Annabella by making her adulterous. Neither argument is unproblematic. Giovanni clearly demonstrates how disordered his sense of morality has become by his assumption that infidelity is worse than incest. He is also presumptuous in insisting that he knows better than the Friar for what sins a person may be damned. Yet, by encouraging marriage, the Friar condones the deception of the bridegroom who will presumably believe that Annabella is chaste. In general, this scene suggests the weakening of the Friar's authority. In his final line, he gives both Annabella and Giovanni up for lost.

QUESTION Giovanni here tries to make a connection between beauty and virtue. Does the play endorse this notion or is beauty represented as something morally dangerous?

QUESTION The Friar exclaims in this scene 'O ignorance in knowledge!' (line 27). Does this judgement apply to Giovanni or might it extend to other characters? How is knowledge represented in another play Ford would have known, Marlowe's *Doctor Faustus*?

GLOSSARY

10 **remarked** singled out

37 **sold to hell** this phrase may deliberately compare Giovanni's plight with that of Dr Faustus with whom Giovanni has some similarities (see **Characterisation: Giovanni**)

44 **shrive her** hear her confession and give her absolution

61 **second death** damnation

SCENE 6

- Annabella rejects Bergetto's proposal of marriage but keeps the jewel Donado gave her.

- Bergetto tells how he was wounded in a fight and was taken in by the doctor, where he met Philotis.

- Giovanni tells Annabella to send back Donado's jewel.

CONTEXT

The ring was understood as a **symbol** not just of the intention to marry but also of female virginity. Annabella's admission that she has given her ring to Giovanni may remind the audience of their sexual union.

Donado gives Annabella the letter he has written on Bergetto's behalf, along with a jewel. Florio suggests that, in return, Annabella should send him the ring intended for her future husband. However, Annabella explains that she no longer has the ring – Giovanni is wearing it – and she proceeds to reject Bergetto's proposal. Bergetto then enters and recounts how he was injured in a quarrel but tended to by the doctor's niece, Philotis, whom he declares to be far prettier than Annabella – Florio hints that she might be a suitable bride for him. Alone with Annabella, Giovanni expresses displeasure at her keeping Donado's jewel. Annabella accuses him of being jealous.

COMMENTARY

Annabella's rejection of Bergetto demonstrates her control over her own marriage arrangements. Not only does her father not rebuke her, he agrees with Giovanni that she has made the right choice. Even Donado commends Annabella for her plain dealing. By contrast, Annabella's relationship with Giovanni looks increasingly complicated. For the first time, this relationship is subtly alluded to and even intrudes upon the question of her marriage. The fact that Annabella has given Giovanni a ring intended for her future husband does not strike Florio as strange, but it reminds the audience of the lovers' persistent definition of their union as a marriage. Where this becomes problematic is the way in which it clearly encourages Giovanni to be proprietorial about Annabella as though she were his wife, so that by the end of the play he is acting the part of the wronged and cuckolded husband. Giovanni already shows signs of jealousy here when he insists that Annabella must not wear the jewel that Donado gave her.

GLOSSARY	
7	cousin a broader term for kinship at this time, here meaning 'nephew'
70	take the wall of me push me away from the wall into the middle of the street, where the drain (*kennel*) ran
93	liked pleased
99	dry severe

ACT III

SCENE 1

- Bergetto describes the presents and kisses that Philotis has given him.
- He then decides to marry her without his uncle's consent.

Having been directed by his uncle in the courtship of Annabella, Bergetto is determined to pursue Philotis himself. He recalls the gifts and the kisses she has given him and asserts that Richardetto has agreed to the marriage. He decides to marry her at once, without his uncle's approval.

COMMENTARY

Bergetto's affection for Philotis is touchingly simple – based on the fact that she has given him a jar of marmalade (any kind of fruit preserve) and a decoration for his cod-piece. These are less expensive but more heartfelt gifts than those with which Donado attempted to woo Annabella and they have considerably more success, perhaps because Philotis and Bergetto act on their own behalf without the intervention of paternal figures. Moreover, although Philotis seems to mother the childish Bergetto, the enthusiasm with which she kisses him and the attention she pays to his codpiece suggest a mutual physical attraction that was certainly absent between Bergetto and Annabella.

CONTEXT

Philotis' name in Greek means 'love' or 'affection'.

GLOSSARY

2	**sconce** brain
3	**bob you off** bribe you with a trivial gift
11	**codpiece-point** lace for fastening the codpiece (pouch that covered the genitals)
14–5	**hugger-mugger** secret
21	**cart whores** prostitutes were publicly shamed by being driven through the streets in a cart. To punish them at one's own expense, as Bergetto imagines his son doing, would suggest one's wealth and concern for public morality

---

SCENE 2

- Soranzo woos Annabella but she mocks him and declines his offer of marriage.

- Giovanni, placed on the balcony above, eavesdrops on their conversation.

- Annabella suddenly feels faint and the doctor is called.

CONTEXT

In the Elizabethan theatre, the figures of Revenge, Love and Fortune were sometimes placed on the balcony to look down on the mortals they were presumed to control. See, for example, *The Rare Triumphs of Love and Fortune* (1582, Anon) or Thomas Kyd's *The Spanish Tragedy* (c. 1587).

Florio tells Soranzo that, despite the financial incentives offered by other suitors, he is Florio's choice as husband for Annabella. His status as a nobleman makes him a good match for a merchant's daughter. Alone together for the first time, Soranzo declares his love for Annabella but she ridicules his courtship and rejects his suit. Giovanni has been listening from above, on the balcony, and is pleased with Annabella's behaviour. She does, however, swear that if she marries anyone it shall be Soranzo. Almost immediately, Annabella falls sick and has to be helped offstage. Soranzo is full of grief, at both her refusal and her sudden illness that he fears may be fatal.

COMMENTARY

Giovanni's position above, listening in to Annabella's courtship by Soranzo, emphasises not only his isolation in the play but also his increasing sense of power. When Annabella argues that the Fates will decide whom she should marry, Giovanni asserts in an aside 'Of those I'm regent now' (line 20) and throughout the rest of the play he will claim the power to control destiny (V.5.11–12). Yet already this assertion sounds like hubris, suggesting that 'pride will come before a fall' and Annabella's sudden illness suggests that he has less control over their affair than he thinks. At this point, Giovanni himself lets out a cry of 'Heaven forbid!' (line 65), suggesting some consciousness on his part that divine providence may now be working to punish them.

Giovanni is also characterised in this scene by a new suspicion and mistrust of Annabella. He slips into conventional misogynistic assumptions such as women are inconstant and they say no when they mean yes (lines 11, 23). This is a far cry from the celestial terms in which he has previously described her, suggesting that Giovanni's idealism may easily turn to cynicism, his love to hatred.

GLOSSARY

5	**jointures** property given to the woman as part of a marriage settlement
11	**be not all woman** i.e. be not inconstant
23	**but one can say that's but a woman's note** only a woman's song, i.e. not the truth
26	**winks** closes her eyes
36	**aqua-vitae** medicinal alcohol

SCENE 3

- Putana tells Giovanni that Annabella is pregnant.

- Giovanni tries to keep the matter a secret.

Putana tells Giovanni that Annabella is not ill but pregnant. To prevent the secret getting out, Giovanni orders her not to let the doctor examine Annabella further. He instructs her to tell Florio that his daughter's sickness was caused by something she ate.

CONTEXT

The symptoms of an illicit pregnancy were often disguised as food-poisoning in plays of this period. Ford may have been thinking of Webster's *The Duchess of Malfi* (1613) in which premature labour is brought on by the eating of apricots.

COMMENTARY

This scene interestingly reverses the balance of power between Giovanni and Putana. It suggests that there is a kind of knowledge that, for once, Giovanni does not possess, but that the female servant does: 'Am I at these years ignorant what the meanings of qualms and water-pangs be, of changing of colours, queasiness of stomachs, of pukings and another thing that I might name?' (lines 10–13). The fact that in the next scene the doctor also seems to be ignorant of what ails Annabella suggests that knowledge is gendered – women know about pregnancy and bodies (partly through necessity); men know about more abstract things such as theology and philosophy. In this instance, Putana's knowledge is seen as being far more useful to Giovanni than his own.

More generally, Annabella's pregnancy is an obvious means by which the secret liaison may now come to light. It suggests that Giovanni and Annabella's belief in their ability to control events and to defy the Heavens has been a fiction – the truth will out and Heaven's revenge for their sin may be beginning to take shape.

GLOSSARY

6	quick pregnant
11	qualms faintness
	water-pangs desire to urinate often
12	another thing i.e. that her periods have stopped
20	take no care not to worry

SCENE 4

- Richardetto tells Florio that Annabella is suffering from a sickness associated with virginity.
- Florio decides to arrange her marriage to Soranzo.
- Giovanni brings the Friar to visit Annabella.

Richardetto tells Florio that there is nothing really wrong with Annabella, attributing her sickness to indigestion from eating melons. Yet he also suggests that she is suffering from an excess of blood, a condition associated with virginity that sex was believed to cure. Without knowing that Annabella has already refused Soranzo, Florio arranges their marriage. He decides that the couple will be betrothed by Friar Bonaventura at his cell. The Friar conveniently appears on the scene, having been brought by Giovanni to hear

Annabella's confession and to give her absolution. Florio asks the Friar to persuade Annabella to agree to the marriage.

COMMENTARY

This scene is full of dramatic irony, mostly at the expense of Florio who may be the only character in the household who does not know that Annabella is pregnant. Richardetto is only posing as a doctor and so the symptoms of pregnancy may have escaped him, but it is also possible that he does know of Annabella's condition and is urging Florio to get her married in order to humiliate his enemy, Soranzo. His allusion to the 'fullness of her blood' (line 8) is both a condition associated with virginity, as Florio understands it, and possibly an allusion to the sexual desire that contributed to her getting pregnant in the first place. Similarly, Giovanni is pretending that he still believes Annabella to be dying and that he has brought the Friar to give her absolution. Ironically, he is congratulated by Florio for showing 'a Christian's care, a brother's love' (line 32).

GLOSSARY	
6	easy surfeit-water mild remedy for indigestion
8	fullness . . . blood i.e. readiness for sex, referred to above as the 'maid's sickness' (III.2.81)
29	ghostly spiritual
35	impression desire

SCENE 5

- Richardetto gives Grimaldi the poison and tells him that Soranzo will be at the Friar's cell.

- Bergetto and Philotis prepare to go to the Friar to be secretly married.

Grimaldi gets ready to kill Soranzo. He knows that it is ignoble of him to win Annabella by killing his rival (and in this underhand way) but he argues that if he cannot win her affections through his own merits then he must use 'policy' (line 5). Richardetto gives Grimaldi the poison and tells him that Annabella and Soranzo are

CONTEXT

The word 'policy' had very negative connotations at this time, being associated with the Italian writer, Niccòlo Machiavelli. In his treatise, *The Prince* (pub. 1532), Machiavelli argued that a ruler should take whatever steps he thinks necessary, however immoral, in order to maintain power.

QUESTION

Disguise was a feature of both comedies and revenge tragedies in this period. How is it used in this play? Is it a kind of deception that is morally justifiable?

to be betrothed in the Friar's cell that night and that he should wait for them there. Richardetto next encounters Bergetto and Philotis who are also planning to marry in secret at the Friar's cell. He applauds their plan but suggests that, in order to avoid discovery, they should travel in disguise.

COMMENTARY

This scene focuses on Richardetto's influence upon the action, beginning with revenge. He provides Grimaldi with poison and tells him where to wait so as to have an opportunity to kill Soranzo. His fantasy of replacing weddings with funerals – 'And they that now dream of a wedding-feast/ May chance to mourn the lusty bridegroom's ruin' (lines 23–4) – makes the connection between weddings and death which is an important motif in the play. More specifically, it anticipates Hippolita's plot in IV.1 where she will attempt to murder Soranzo on his actual wedding-day.

Ironically, at the same time, Richardetto is also arranging the marriage of his niece. We discover in this scene that Philotis has been urged by her uncle to love Bergetto (lines 27–8) though Ford never provides Richardetto with a motive for this. We might assume that Bergetto's wealth is a major factor. Perhaps harder to comprehend is why Richardetto should be so keen for the couple to marry on the same night and in the same place as Soranzo and Annabella when he knows that a murderer will be lurking in the vicinity.

The main function of the scene is to set up the threat to both couples represented by Grimaldi as he waits outside the Friar's cell.

GLOSSARY		
7	play not on both hands	act deceitfully
9	affied	betrothed
31	call his coz to shrift	make his kinsman repent
36	buss	kiss

SCENE 6

- The Friar persuades Annabella to repent her sins and marry Soranzo.
- Soranzo and Annabella are betrothed by the Friar in the presence of Giovanni, Florio and Vasques.

The scene begins with Annabella weeping as the Friar describes the torments of hell that she will suffer unless she asks Heaven's forgiveness of her sins. Being assured of her repentance, he urges Annabella to marry Soranzo to preserve her reputation but insists that she must give up Giovanni. Annabella reluctantly agrees. The Friar joins Soranzo and Annabella's hands together. The marriage ceremony will be performed later.

COMMENTARY

The Friar seems to fulfil his spiritual duty here by frightening Annabella into repentance and persuading her to renounce incest. Yet his recommendation that she should marry is morally dubious. Even if Annabella keeps her promise to remain faithful to Soranzo, she marries him under false pretences for Soranzo will presumably believe her unborn child to be his own. The Friar's plan suggests that he is more concerned with social status and reputation than we might expect of a religious man, reminding us of his more worldly role as a university tutor and of the conflict of loyalties he has already experienced in relation to Giovanni.

We might also question the Friar's insistence that Annabella is more to blame than her brother. He imagines Giovanni as one of the souls in hell, crying 'O, would my wicked sister/ Had first been damned, when she did yield to lust!' (lines 29–30) and uses this image to make Annabella more contrite. This assumption that female rather than male lust is responsible for the tragedy is repeated at the end of the play by the Cardinal.

GLOSSARY

6	**read a lecture** deliver a moralising speech
9	**List** listen

CONTEXT
The Friar's joining of Annabella and Soranzo's hands, in the presence of a witness, was called 'hand-fasting' and was legally binding (see **Themes: Marriage**).

CHECK THE BOOK
The Friar's description of hell derives from a prose fiction by Thomas Nashe called *Pierce Penniless* (1592). Ford had borrowed it once already in a poem he published entitled *Christ's Bloody Sweat* (1613).

QUESTION
The Friar appears to blame Annabella more than Giovanni at this stage. Do you think Ford is seeking to expose the unfair treatment of women by religion and society, or to reinforce these values?

CONTEXT

Ford's play was written for The Phoenix, an indoor theatre in Drury Lane in London, also known as The Cockpit. Here, all the lighting would have been provided by candles, thus allowing for real darkness during this scene.

SCENE 7

- Grimaldi kills Bergetto, having mistaken him for Soranzo.

Grimaldi lies in wait for Soranzo but in the dark, hearing a man address a woman as 'sweetheart' (line 4), he mistakenly stabs Bergetto. Bergetto dies, to the great grief of Philotis and his servant, Poggio.

COMMENTARY

The excitement of this scene depends partly on the fact that it happens in semi-darkness. For the audience, as for the characters, the confusion is only resolved when lights are brought on and the extent of Bergetto's blood loss is revealed.

Bergetto's murder is partly a matter of chance. It is unfortunate that he should be where Grimaldi expects Soranzo and that he should identify himself as a lover through the endearment 'sweetheart' (line 4). Yet Ford may be making a larger point. Before Grimaldi strikes, he cries: 'Now guide my hand, some angry Justice,/ Home to his bosom' (lines 6–7). The results of his action suggest either that it would not be justice for Grimaldi to kill Soranzo or that Justice is not available to respond. Both arguments have some weight. Grimaldi confesses here, as he did in III.5, that his motive for wanting Soranzo dead is weak. More suggestive, however, is the idea that Justice has fled from the earth. This was a common complaint in revenge tragedies, where the **protagonist** turns to violence because he cannot get justice (see **Dramatic genre: Revenge tragedy**). This is, then, one of the darkest scenes of the play, literally and figuratively. It suggests that there may not be any divine providence guiding the mortals' actions and that Bergetto's death is meaningless.

GLOSSARY

1	*dark lantern* lantern where the light could be closed off, associated with criminals
8	flesh-tailor surgeon
27	linen petticoats

SCENE 8

- Vasques tells Hippolita about Soranzo's marriage and she plots her revenge.

Vasques tells Hippolita that Soranzo and Annabella are already betrothed and that the marriage will happen in two days. Hippolita vows to kill Soranzo on his wedding-day but warns that her success will depend on the loyalty of Vasques. Vasques reassures her that he would hardly miss out on such an opportunity for self-advancement.

QUESTION
Why do you think Hippolita needs Vasques' help? Does Ford want her to appear reliant on another man?

COMMENTARY

The tension in the play is starting to mount as we are given a time-frame for Hippolita's revenge, following immediately after Grimaldi's failed attempt to kill Soranzo. There is no hint that Vasques is not fully on Hippolita's side.

GLOSSARY

17–18	my youth . . . pleasures this could refer to either Soranzo or Vasques

SCENE 9

- Donado, Florio and Richardetto lament Bergetto's death.
- They discover that the murderer was Grimaldi and that he fled to the house of the Cardinal.
- The Cardinal refuses to deliver Grimaldi to the law and instead sends him to Rome.

The play's father-figures – Donado, Florio and Richardetto – lament Bergetto's murder and decide to pursue justice. They have been told that Grimaldi fled to the house of the Cardinal and they go there to ask for him to be handed over to the law. The Cardinal, however, refuses, arguing that because Grimaldi is a nobleman he should be treated more leniently and he sends him into the protection of the Pope in Rome. Donado complains about this

CHECK THE BOOK

A famous precedent for this debate is found in Kyd's *The Spanish Tragedy*. The **protagonist**, Hieronimo, whose son has been murdered, deliberates whether or not to take revenge: '*Vindicta mihi!* [Revenge is mine]/ Ay, Heaven will be revenged of every ill,/ Nor will they suffer murder unrepaid' (III.13.1–3). Unlike Donado, however, Hieronimo does proceed to take revenge.

abuse of justice. Florio agrees but urges patience for 'there's no help in this/ When cardinals think murder's not amiss' (lines 66–7). He promises Donado that Heaven will be revenged.

COMMENTARY

This scene sharply defines the distinctions of class that have only been hinted at so far in the play. Donado, Florio and Richardetto may be wealthy, upright citizens of Parma but they are not noble or aristocratic. For this reason, the Cardinal speaks to them contemptuously and protects the now penitent murderer, Grimaldi, simply because he is 'nobly born/ Of princes' blood' (lines 56–7). Indeed, the Cardinal implies that Florio was partly to blame by refusing to support Grimaldi's offer of marriage, sarcastically suggesting that Florio thought him 'too mean [low-born] a husband for your daughter' (line 58).

The emphasis on justice being unavailable echoes the conclusion of Act III Scene 7 that 'Justice is fled to Heaven and comes no nearer' (III.7.63), but whilst this might have served as the motive for a revenge-plot, here the action is pursued no further. Rather than Donado mounting his own retaliation against Grimaldi, he and the other men accept that Heaven will take revenge for them. Whilst this makes for a rather anti-climactic plot, it does emphasise the difference between the younger generation in the play – Grimaldi, Soranzo and Giovanni – who care more for revenge than justice, and the older generation who refuse to transgress against the law and who meet adversity with patience. The only exception to this rule is Richardetto whose actions have indirectly led to Bergetto's murder. Possibly he should also be played as one of the younger men of the play, even though he has an adult niece. Yet, in Act IV Scene 2, he too will renounce revenge.

GLOSSARY	
1	**bootless** pointless
28	**mates** suggests they are lower class, deliberately insulting
60	**wit** common sense

ACT IV

SCENE 1

- After the marriage of Annabella and Soranzo has been performed, the couple celebrate with a banquet.
- Hippolita appears with other ladies to perform a masque for their entertainment.
- She gives Soranzo a poisoned drink but is tricked by Vasques into drinking it herself and dies.

The Friar opens the scene by declaring Annabella and Soranzo officially married and the celebrations begin with a banquet. An unexpected entertainment is announced in the form of masked women, dressed in white and carrying willow branches, who perform a dance. At the end, one of them reveals herself to be Hippolita. She insists that her intent is to be reconciled with the couple and she joins their hands, releasing Soranzo from all the oaths he had made to her and offering a toast. Vasques hands her a cup of wine from which she drinks and Soranzo is about to drink too when Vasques stops him. He reveals the details of Hippolita's attempt to kill Soranzo which has resulted only in her own poisoning. With her last breath, Hippolita curses Soranzo and Annabella: 'May thy bed/ Of marriage be a rack unto thy heart . . . May'st thou live/ To father bastards, may her womb bring forth/ Monsters' (lines 91–2, 94–5). The Friar points out the moral of the tragedy to Giovanni, warning that lust will be punished, and that a marriage that begins with such violence is surely doomed.

COMMENTARY

This scene represents a sensational reversal of expectations: a wedding-day, intended to celebrate love and social harmony, is dramatically transformed into a scene of vengeance and death. This kind of juxtaposition was a favourite technique of Ford's (see **Critical approaches: Structure**), but it is also particularly appropriate to *'Tis Pity She's a Whore* in which love and hatred are consistently related. The scene is full of hints that appearances are

CONTEXT

This reference to 'Monsters' recalls the fact that the children of siblings have a greater risk of genetic abnormality, but it also alludes to the illegitimacy of Giovanni and Annabella's child. '[B]astards', the offspring of an unlawful union, were often presumed to be unnatural or monstrous.

CHECK THE BOOK
In Shakespeare's *Much Ado About Nothing* (1600), Claudio praises Hero: 'Can the world buy such a jewel?' (I.1.171). Once he believes her to have lost her virginity, however, she loses all her value, becoming no better in his eyes than a prostitute or 'common stale' (III.5.65).

not what they seem. Soranzo is overjoyed to have won Annabella, 'this most precious jewel' (line 10). Yet an audience knows that she is only marrying him because she is pregnant. 'Jewel' was a common **metaphor** for woman's virginity – a treasure that Annabella lost a long time ago. Also **ironic** is the fact that Soranzo celebrates his recent delivery from Grimaldi's attempt against his life. Again, an audience knows that it is on this very day that Hippolita has promised to kill him. Whilst Soranzo celebrates his wedding, we are anticipating his death.

The convention of celebrating an aristocratic wedding through a performance by masked dancers enables Hippolita secretly to gain access to her intended victim. However, it also serves the interest of Hippolita's own reputation, again to ironic effect. White was symbolic of chastity and the dancers are described as 'certain young maidens of Parma' (line 30) implying that they are all virgins, including Hippolita. Moreover, by carrying willow, a symbol of forsaken love, Hippolita insists that the blame lies entirely with Soranzo. Thus, the masque attempts to restore Hippolita's reputation, even as it is the means by which she intends to commit murder.

The failure of this plot strikes the onlookers with wonder. It suggests that justice is still possible on earth; that Heaven is working towards the destruction of evil by thwarting Hippolita's scheme. Perhaps the chief significance of the scene, however, is the way in which it anticipates what will happen to Annabella and Giovanni. The Friar points out: 'that marriage's seldom good/ Where the bride-banquet so begins in blood' (lines 107–8). This is a ludicrous statement if you think about it – when did the Friar last attend a celebration that included murder? If such marriages seldom go well, does that mean that he has known marriages that did endure such a bloody start? Still, the play will prove that the Friar is right to consider Annabella and Soranzo's marriage to be doomed. More importantly, the actions of Hippolita and the punishment she receives also anticipate the fate of Giovanni. Hippolita kills Soranzo because she is angry at his betrayal and jealous of the woman who has displaced her as his bride. Similarly, Giovanni is increasingly jealous of Soranzo, Annabella's new husband, and he fantasises about the violent acts he would perform to avoid the sight of 'my love/ Clipped by another' (lines 16–17).

Hippolita's frustrated love that turns to hate anticipates the way in which Giovanni's love of Annabella will lead him to kill both her and her husband. The Friar warns Giovanni to pay close attention to what has happened, intending it as a lesson on the punishment of lust. For an audience, it is equally a warning against the violence inspired by lust.

CHECK THE BOOK

In *Othello* (1603), Desdemona sings a famous 'willow song' about a woman who is forsaken by her lover (IV.3). The fact that Desdemona is killed shortly afterwards may anticipate Hippolita's imminent death in this scene. See also *Hamlet* (IV.7), where Gertrude tells of Ophelia's suicide in a place where 'a willow grows aslant a brook'.

GLOSSARY		
19	**wait** perform your duties as an attendant
32	**masque** an entertainment by masked performers, featuring singing and dancing, often performed at aristocratic weddings
37	*willow* symbol of unrequited or forsaken love
55	**engaged us** placed us in your debt
56	**single** sincere
	charity unselfish love
57	**remit** renounce
71	*Troppo . . . inganna* 'To hope too much deceives' (Italian)
82	**she hath yet . . .** the rest of this line is missing

SCENE 2

- Richardetto decides to abandon his revenge against Soranzo.
- Philotis is sent to a nunnery.

Having been powerfully impressed by the events at the marriage-feast, Richardetto decides to abandon his own revenge plot against Soranzo, believing that 'There is one/Above begins to work' (lines 8–9). Rumour has it that there is already trouble in the marriage between Soranzo and Annabella. In order to protect his niece from whatever danger will ensue, Richardetto sends Philotis to become a nun, asking her to pray for him.

COMMENTARY

This scene represents another premature ending to a revenge plot, with one of the key players, Richardetto, quitting his role in the belief that Heaven is doing his work for him. Although Richardetto

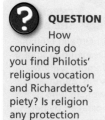

QUESTION

How convincing do you find Philotis' religious vocation and Richardetto's piety? Is religion any protection against disaster in the play?

never seemed to have revenge planned for his wife, the fact that Heaven has taken this out of his hands makes a deep impression on him. The result is that he will try to protect his niece, Philotis, from being further embroiled in a place so dangerous as Parma. He will also keep her sexually pure since lust was apparently Hippolita's downfall (as it may yet prove to be Annabella's). Philotis' acquiescence to life as a nun seems rather unconvincing, given the lustiness with which she kissed Bergetto and her apparent eagerness to be married. This decision seems more indicative of Richardetto's new religious convictions than of anything Philotis feels.

GLOSSARY		
12	slightens	scorns
18	votaress	nun
26	beads	rosary beads

SCENE 3

- Having discovered that Annabella is pregnant, Soranzo confronts her and vows to take revenge.

- Vasques tricks Putana into revealing that Giovanni is the father of Annabella's child.

In a furious rage, Soranzo drags a visibly pregnant Annabella on to the stage and accuses her of being a whore. He is desperate to discover the identity of the baby's father but Annabella asserts that she would rather die than tell him. Vasques enters and rebukes his master's cruelty, but in an aside to Soranzo, he urges him to delay his revenge until Vasques has found out the truth. Soranzo concurs and dissolves into tears, promising to forgive his wife if she will subsequently be faithful to him. He sends her into her chamber. Vasques then encounters Putana, weeping, and persuades her to reveal the identity of Annabella's lover. As soon as she names Giovanni, Vasques orders a band of rogues (*banditti*) to seize Putana, tie her up, gag her and take her offstage to be blinded. Soranzo re-enters and Vasques prepares to tell him the truth.

COMMENTARY

Although in this scene Annabella appears to be in a vulnerable and weak position, she also shows great strength. Her refusal to name her lover, despite the threat against her life, is courageous, though the recklessness with which she antagonises Soranzo suggests she might actually wish to die. By contrast, Soranzo, for all his physical power, is revealed to be comparatively helpless. He cannot make Annabella disclose the truth, he can only 'rip up [her] heart and find it there' (lines 53–4). This threat anticipates Giovanni's displaying of Annabella's heart in the final scene, suggesting that male violence in this play is an expression of frustration at the impossibility not only of controlling women but of really understanding them. Soranzo's subsequent change of attitude to Annabella – from anger to passionate love and sorrow – is feigned. Yet in his pretence at grief we may glimpse another aspect of his character – not just the heartless playboy who betrayed Hippolita but someone genuinely infatuated. He describes Annabella as a 'saint' whom he 'did too superstitiously adore' (lines 111 and 119), implying that his love is a form of idolatry.

The tone of the scene changes abruptly, however, with Vasques' deception of Putana, demonstrating the sharply conflicting sympathies that the play as a whole produces. We may admire Vasques' ingenuity in tricking Putana, a character who is defined not only by her naivety but by the self-interest which urges her to betray the lovers. Vasques promises that she will gain 'everlasting love and preferment' (line 202), 'You shall be rewarded' (line 209). Nevertheless, the punishment of Putana is so gratuitous and extreme, and inspires such glee in Vasques, that our sympathies shift again. When he cries out 'O horrible!' (line 234) he is referring to the discovery of incest, but an audience is surely thinking of Putana's fate.

CHECK THE BOOK

Soranzo's confrontation with Annabella recalls the famous closet scene between Hamlet and his mother, Gertrude. Both men agree on woman's frailty, by which they mean her capacity for sexual betrayal ('*Tis Pity She's a Whore* IV.3.144–5 and *Hamlet* I.2.146). (See also **Extended commentaries: Text 2**).

CONTEXT

Idolatry was a crime punished by death in the Bible (*Deuteronomy*, chapter 4). Moreover, Renaissance physicians often warned against the dangers of immoderate love, leading the victim to madness and suicide.

GLOSSARY

SD	*unbraced*	not properly dressed
6	bawd	pimp
8	pleurisy	either a disease characterised by fever or excess
9	heyday of your luxury	highpoint of sexual excitement

continued

QUESTION
Does the play suggest any consistent attitude towards violence, either condemnatory or admiring? Are our attitudes towards violence likely to be different to those of Ford's original audience?

GLOSSARY

10	**surfeit** excessive amount (that finally causes disgust)
11	**close** secret
13	**gallimaufry** mixture i.e. the illegitimate child
16	**sued not to** wooed
20	**would . . . doing** wouldn't wait (with sexual **pun** suggesting that Soranzo was eager to 'do' Annabella himself)
25	**quean** woman who is sexually promiscuous
29	**stay . . . stomach** satisfy your appetite. Here Soranzo is imagined as the one suffering from pregnancy cravings, though for information not food
35	**a match** it's a deal
47	**that you had been a creature** that you existed
59	*Che morte . . . amore* (Italian) 'What death is sweeter than to die for love?'
61	**lust-belepered** made leprous by lust
63	*Morendo . . . dolore* (Italian) 'Dying in favour with him, I would die without pain'
76	**slack** delay
78	**forfend** forbid
119	**superstitiously** blasphemously, as though she were an idol
126	**humorous** changeable
152	**great in the stock** pregnant
154	**cunny-berry** rabbit-hole i.e. vagina
163	**the nonce** now, the present
170	**up . . . quick** both terms for pregnant
219	**a Turk or a Jew** proverbial for a dishonest un-Christian person
222	*Banditti* gang of Italian robbers
237–8	**how a smooth tale . . . smooth tail** how a lie overcomes a woman, tail meaning vagina
249	**liberality** generous tipping
264	**gain glory of** overcome

ACT V

SCENE 1

- Annabella, imprisoned in her chamber, writes a letter in her own blood to warn Giovanni.
- The Friar finds the letter and promises to deliver it.

CHECK THE BOOK

Annabella's act of writing a letter in blood and dropping it from her balcony is an obvious borrowing from Kyd's *The Spanish Tragedy* in which Bel-Imperia performs the same actions.

Annabella appears on the balcony, having been locked into her chamber by Soranzo. She has written a letter in her own blood (presumably ink has been denied to her), confessing her sins and warning Giovanni not to trust Soranzo. She lets the letter fall from the balcony hoping that someone will pass by and deliver it. The Friar overhears her confession of guilt and rejoices. He agrees to deliver the letter.

COMMENTARY

Just when a repentant Annabella is thinking of the Friar, he suddenly appears. This might look like a coincidence but in the increasingly devout world of the play it is greeted as a sign of Heaven's intervention. The Friar says, 'Lady, Heaven hath heard you,/ And hath by providence ordained that I/ Should be his minister . . .' (lines 37–9). Also worth noting is the way in which Annabella blames herself for their predicament. She wishes that Giovanni had been 'less subject to those stars/ That luckless reigned at my nativity!' (lines 19–20), and laments the consequences of her crime, not his: 'O, would the scourge due to my black offence/ Might pass from thee . . . ' (lines 21–2). Clearly, Annabella was struck by the Friar's suggestion in III.6 that she was more to blame than her brother. Yet she attains a kind of heroism in this scene, spilling her blood in order to warn Giovanni and briefly making herself the tragic protagonist who bestows on future ages, 'A wretched, woeful woman's tragedy' (line 8).

GLOSSARY	
1	**thriftless** pointless
14	**turtle** turtle-dove, associated with faithful love

CONTEXT

In the early modern period Italians were often stereotyped as particularly jealous husbands. In Ben Jonson's play, *Volpone* (1605), a comedy set in Venice, the husband Corvino threatens to kill his wife's 'father, mother, brother, all thy race' if she proves unfaithful (II.5.27–9).

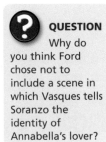

QUESTION

Why do you think Ford chose not to include a scene in which Vasques tells Soranzo the identity of Annabella's lover?

SCENE 2

- Vasques taunts Soranzo with his wife's infidelity and urges him to take revenge.

- Soranzo tells Vasques to invite guests including Giovanni and Florio to a birthday-feast.

Vasques reminds Soranzo of all the crimes committed against him by Annabella and urges him to be resolute in his revenge. Soranzo says that he will have her put on her wedding-dress and that he will invite her father and brother to a feast to celebrate his birthday. Reference is made to their employing *banditti*, a band of violent thugs, though their purpose is not yet explained.

COMMENTARY

This scene demonstrates Vasques' increasing prominence in the plotting and execution of his master's revenge. Despite Soranzo's tendency to violent anger earlier in the play, here he appears susceptible to pity, an emotion that Vasques fears will deflect them from their purpose. Thus Vasques encourages Soranzo to be angry (where before he had urged him to be patient) by dwelling upon Annabella's lust and her betrayal.

Exactly what kind of revenge Soranzo is planning for Annabella remains unclear. The idea that she should appear in her wedding-dress before the other guests, including her father, suggests that Soranzo intends to repudiate his bride in public. This was not without dramatic precedent. In Shakespeare's comedy *Much Ado about Nothing*, Claudio waits until the middle of the wedding ceremony to cast off Hero as an unchaste bride. However, Ford may also have been thinking of a Shakespearean tragedy here (see **Literary background: Ford and Shakespeare**). In *Othello*, we find the same division of roles. The faithful sidekick (Iago/Vasques) will kill the adulterer (Cassio/Giovanni) whilst the wronged husband kills his wife. The fact that Soranzo wants Annabella dressed in her wedding-dress recalls the fact that on the night of her murder Desdemona asks for the wedding-sheets to be laid on the bed. Moreover, Soranzo's promise that he will 'Kiss her and fold her gently in my arms' (line 11), echoes Othello's kissing and then suffocation of Desdemona.

> **GLOSSARY**
>
> 2   **horns** a sign of being a cuckold (see below)
>
> 3   **cuckold you** make you into a cuckold i.e. a man whose wife has been unfaithful to him
>
> 4   **pander** pimp

SCENE 3

- Giovanni argues that Annabella's marriage has made no difference to his relationship with her.

- The Friar delivers Annabella's letter but Giovanni refuses to believe its contents.

- Vasques invites Giovanni to Soranzo's birthday feast and he accepts, despite the Friar's warnings.

> **CONTEXT**
>
> Marlowe's Dr Faustus also famously declares 'Come, I think hell's a fable' (I.5.130). Yet Faustus quickly finds the truth of hell, as Ford suggests Giovanni will.

Giovanni describes in **soliloquy** how Annabella's marriage has made no difference to their relationship. They take as much pleasure in one another sexually as before. He insists that he would rather have this happiness on earth than the promise of Heaven and denies that hell even exists.

The Friar enters and delivers Annabella's letter but Giovanni refuses to believe that they are discovered. He blames Annabella for being a coward and even accuses the Friar of having forged the letter. Vasques now enters and invites Giovanni to Soranzo's feast. The Friar urges him not to go but Giovanni insists. The Friar now abandons all hope of saving Giovanni and decides to leave Parma.

COMMENTARY

Giovanni's appearance alone on stage again suggests his isolation within the play. His belief that he is unaffected by other people's actions and invulnerable to their threats has serious implications in this scene. For a start, he cannot believe that anyone could have found out his and Annabella's secret, although news of trouble in the marriage had reached Richardetto some time ago (Act IV Scene 2). He also refuses to accept the Friar's warning against going to Soranzo's birthday celebration. There is something arrogant and foolhardy in Giovanni's refusal to listen to advice or to act cautiously. He seems to rush headlong into catastrophe. Yet there is also something heroic in his determination not to be a victim. At the end of the scene, he begins to shape his own plot to seize control of the action away from Soranzo although he seems remarkably unconcerned about whom exactly he will destroy in the process: 'If I must totter like a well-grown oak,/ Some undershrubs shall in my weighty fall/ Be crushed to splits; with me they all shall perish' (lines 77–9).

GLOSSARY		
17	jubilee	celebration
18	retired	private
28	factor	intermediary
39	dotage	stupidity/confusion associated with old age
72	set up my rest	played my last hand (in a card game)
73	baneful	dire
75	prescription	custom/morality
79	splits	splinters

SCENE 4

- Soranzo gives the *banditti* money to commit murder and promises them a pardon.

- Giovanni arrives and is sent in to Annabella's chamber.

- The other guests arrive, including the Cardinal, Florio and Donado.

Vasques and Soranzo brief the *banditti* on the murder they are about to perform, urging them to 'be bloody enough and . . . unmerciful' (line 3). Soranzo pays them and promises that they will be pardoned (*banditti* were often men who had been banished from society).

Once the *banditti* have gone, Vasques urges Soranzo to go through with his revenge against Annabella. He suggests that when

CONTEXT

In Thomas Nashe's fictional travel narrative, *The Unfortunate Traveller* (1594), 'bandittos' are described as 'certain outlaws that lie betwixt Rome and Naples, and besiege the passage, so that none can travel that way without robbing. Now and then, hired for some few crowns, they will steal to Rome and do a murder, and betake them to their heels again. Disguised as they go, they are not known from strangers; sometimes they will shroud themselves under the habit of grave citizens'.

Giovanni arrives he should be encouraged to go into Annabella's chamber where he may try to have sex with her, thus allowing him to be killed in an act of sin that would ensure his damnation. The guests arrive and Giovanni goes into Annabella's chamber.

COMMENTARY

Although the *banditti* have now been paid upfront for the murder and they know their cue, the final details of Giovanni's death are still being agreed. For example, it is not enough that Giovanni should die, he must also be damned, hence Vasques' suggestion that they kill him in the very act of committing incest. It may seem absurd to imagine that if Giovanni and Annabella are left alone in her chamber they will have sex, with the birthday preparations going on outside. Yet Giovanni's lustful **soliloquy** in the previous scene and his recklessness seem to allow this as a possibility.

What is notable about Soranzo in this scene is his uncertainty and his reliance on Vasques for reassurance. He asks the *banditti*: 'You will not fail, or shrink in the attempt?' (line 1) and then 'The guests will all come, Vasques?' (line 19). Clearly, Soranzo is nervous as the time for revenge draws near and this is why Vasques must once again remind him of Annabella's crimes. In the event, we never find out if Soranzo would have kept his nerve when confronted with Annabella. Vasques' deployment of the *banditti* looks more and more like a means of his avoiding too great a reliance on Soranzo's capacity for vengeance. Dramatically, the *banditti* also ensure that Giovanni rather than Soranzo remains the play's principal revenger.

CHECK THE BOOK

Vasques' damnation fantasy is clearly borrowed from Shakespeare's *Hamlet*. In that play, Hamlet plans to kill his uncle when the latter is having sex with Gertrude to ensure that he goes to hell.

GLOSSARY	
5	Liguria mountainous region near Parma
10	all free the *banditti* are presumably exiles for whom pardons might be secured to make them citizens once again
12	vizard mask
31	hare renowned for its sexual appetite
	law a head-start

SCENE 5

- Annabella warns Giovanni that Soranzo is preparing to take his revenge.
- Giovanni makes Annabella pray for forgiveness of her sins, kisses her and then stabs her to death.

Giovanni refuses to take Annabella's repentance seriously and condemns her inconstancy to their 'vows and oaths' (line 5). Annabella warns him of the dangers to come and urges him to escape. Weeping now, Giovanni urges her to pray for forgiveness of her sins, and kisses her repeatedly. Then he stabs her to death. He leaves the stage with her body, promising to perform some 'last and greater part' (line 107).

COMMENTARY

Giovanni's murder of Annabella is shocking because, unlike all the other deaths in the play, we have very little preparation for it. Where Soranzo's revenge has been gradually building, Giovanni acts impulsively and without having taken the audience into his confidence, despite his habit for asides and soliloquies. His actions within this scene prepare us to some extent – he weeps and describes his tears as 'funeral tears/ Shed on your grave' (lines 49–50); he imagines Annabella going ahead of him to Heaven; he urges her to pray so that she is ready for death. Moreover, the parallels with *Othello* (see **Literary background: Ford and Shakespeare**) create a strong sense of foreboding. Still, the fact that Annabella is taken by surprise allows the audience some excuse for its shock. She is prepared for death but expects either to take her own life or to succumb to Soranzo's plot but not to be killed by Giovanni: 'O, brother, by your hand?' (line 87).

A variety of motives are offered for Giovanni's killing of Annabella. He describes it as an act of love and a kind of martyrdom, as though he were trying to spare her from disgrace or contamination, much as Richardetto has spared Philotis by sending her to the nunnery. Yet he kills her with the words 'Revenge is mine' (line 86), as if punishing her for her supposed betrayal.

CHECK THE FILM

Giuseppe Patroni Griffi's film (1973) of *'Tis Pity She's a Whore* makes it clear that Annabella knows what is coming and is complicit in her own death. Charlotte Rampling, playing Annabella, bears her breast for Oliver Tobias' (Giovanni's) dagger. She places her hand on the dagger and Giovanni places his on top, in a visual echo of their vow to love or kill one another earlier in the film.

Similarly, 'Honour doth love command' (line 86) implies that he is playing the role of Othello, that is, the jealous husband rebuking his adulterous wife, but in fact it is Soranzo who is the wronged husband and Giovanni who is the adulterer. Finally, and perhaps most disturbingly, Giovanni seems to be motivated by male competitiveness: 'Soranzo, thou hast missed thy aim in this:/ I have prevented now thy reaching plots . . .' (lines 100–1). Our final impression is of Giovanni as a man whose judgement is fundamentally impaired. His act of murder does not have the meaning for anyone else that it has for him.

> **GLOSSARY**
> 2   night-games sexual intercourse
> 11   bent brows frown
> 27   harbinger forerunner or omen
> 77   cunning flattery i.e. her hands give the illusion of health when she is actually on the point of death
> 82   Styx river in the classical underworld whose waters were black

SCENE 6

- Giovanni bursts on to the banquet scene bearing a heart on the end of his dagger and explains that it belongs to Annabella, who was pregnant by him. Florio falls down dead with shock.

- Giovanni stabs Soranzo who shortly after dies. Vasques and Giovanni fight and Giovanni is wounded. Vasques calls 'Vengeance' and the *banditti* enter and kill Giovanni.

- The Cardinal orders that Putana be burnt for her crimes and that Vasques be banished. He seizes the wealth of Florio and of Soranzo.

- Richardetto reveals his identity. The characters leave the stage to discuss the tragedy further.

 CHECK THE NET
You can find several reviews of recent productions of the play online. Try typing ''Tis Pity She's a Whore review' into your search engine.

Into the middle of the birthday banquet bursts Giovanni, covered in blood and carrying a dagger with a human heart on the end. The characters cannot understand what this means despite Giovanni's repeated attempts at explanation. Finally, he makes them understand that the heart belonged to his sister, Annabella, with whom he has been sexually involved for the past nine months. He reveals that she became pregnant and that he has killed both mother and unborn child. Vasques is sent offstage to find out if this is true and returns to confirm it, having presumably seen what remains of the body. Florio falls dead on the spot. Soranzo begins to rebuke Giovanni but is stabbed by him and dies. Vasques intervenes and wounds Giovanni. He also gives the signal at which the *banditti* enter and they give Giovanni his death-wound. Giovanni dies, unrepentant, hoping only to see Annabella's face again in the afterlife. The Cardinal demands an explanation from Vasques who insists that he acted entirely out of loyalty to his master, Soranzo. He reveals that Putana was also in on the secret and the Cardinal orders that she be taken outside the city and burnt. Vasques is banished from Parma. The Cardinal then seizes all the wealth and property belonging to the dead for the Church's use. Richardetto steps in at this point and reveals his true identity. He offers to explain in greater detail what he has seen of this revenge tragedy. The characters leave the stage with the Cardinal's final comment on Annabella: ''Tis pity she's a whore' (line 159).

COMMENTARY

Giovanni's visual appearance on stage is horrifying enough, even before the characters have worked out what it means. The fact that it takes them so long to understand that the heart belongs to Annabella is partly a testament to the fact that, for all its meaning for Giovanni, the heart is just a piece of flesh with no characteristics that anyone else can comprehend (see **Extended commentaries: Text 3**), and partly the fact that despite its street-brawls, Parma is totally unused to such extreme displays of violence. Incest, too, is unthinkable and the shock of this discovery kills Florio instantly.

Soranzo's response when he first sees Giovanni is to assume correctly that the latter has seized the initiative for revenge and that he has been 'forestalled' (line 15). Even so, Soranzo still tries to get his own revenge back on track. Unable to comprehend that Annabella is really dead, he asks for her to be brought out on stage: 'Bring the strumpet forth!' (line 54), presumably so that he can kill her in public as he had planned. Not only is this now impossible, but Soranzo himself is fatally wounded before the *banditti* can arrive. Only Giovanni, it seems, is quite satisfied with the way events have fallen out, for he has dominated the revenge tragedy and upstaged Soranzo. Although he is killed by Vasques and the *banditti*, he insists that he always intended to die: 'I thank thee: thou hast done for me/ But what I would have else done on myself' (lines 97–8).

At the end of the play, justice is seen to take over from revenge. Donado calls the death of Giovanni, a 'strange miracle of justice' (line 108). The Cardinal deploys legal redress – public execution and banishment – against the remaining criminals, Putana and Vasques.

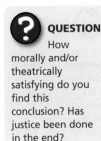

QUESTION

How morally and/or theatrically satisfying do you find this conclusion? Has justice been done in the end?

GLOSSARY		
6	cause	good reason
10	trimmed	covered/decorated
19	rape	violent theft
39	moons	months
48	bewrayed	disclosed
143	dispense	commute the sentence
144	reason	motive

EXTENDED COMMENTARIES

TEXT 1 – I.2.204–62 (PP. 61–3)

From 'here's my breast' to 'kiss and sleep'.

Before the passage begins, Giovanni has decided to confess his feelings to Annabella. He begins by praising her beauty but finds that she will not take him seriously. Hence, he suddenly offers her his dagger, pointed towards his breast, so that she may prove the truth of his words.

Giovanni's offer to show Annabella his heart (lines 205–6) reflects an assumption that recurs throughout the play, namely that when exposed to the spectator's view the human heart will reveal its possessor's secrets. This was partly a metaphor from romantic

CHECK THE BOOK

Sir Philip Sidney's **sonnet sequence**, *Astrophil and Stella* (1581–3) makes repeated use of this heart imagery. In Sonnet I, the Muse tells Astrophil to 'Look in thy heart and write'. In Sonnet IV, Astrophil offers to prove his love: 'I swear, my heart such one shall show to thee . . .'

poetry, according to which the lover carried an image of his mistress in his heart. At the same time, since literally showing someone else your heart would probably lead to your death, such a promise also suggested a man's sincerity. Giovanni insists that he would reveal the truth to Annabella: 'though my heart/ Were rated at the price of that attempt' (lines 157–8). Finally, this act of displaying the heart recalls the practice of public executions in the seventeenth century. Particularly in cases of treason, the executioner would hold out the criminal's heart for the public to inspect since it was assumed that treachery (as well as love) could be written there. In the final scene, Annabella's heart is displayed to prove both her love and her treachery to Giovanni (see **Extended commentaries: Text 3**).

More generally, there is a powerful sense of emotional release in Giovanni's words and actions here. Where in the first scene he 'unclasped [his] burdened soul' (line 13) to the Friar, now he threatens to rip open his breast in order to release 'the hidden flames/ That almost have consumed me' (lines 217–18). The physical and emotional constraint recommended by the Friar is now giving way to a kind of reckless freedom. But if Giovanni confesses in the hope of a better life, his love for Annabella is also inextricably linked to a desire for death. He describes the torments of his love as potentially fatal (line 209) and he is clearly suicidal when he bids her strike him in line 214. At other times, Giovanni imagines death as the solution to his suffering if she will not return his affection: ''tis my destiny/ That you must either love or I must die' (lines 223–4). This connection between love and death continues through the rest of the scene. Even when Annabella admits her love, raising Giovanni from gloomy despair to transcendent joy, the couple's love remains (to quote *Romeo and Juliet*) 'death-marked' (Prologue, line 9). They invent vows that recall the marriage ceremony by promising to love one another until death, but more sinisterly, they suggest that the end of love will be fatal: 'Do not betray me to your mirth or hate/ Love me or kill me . . . ' (lines 250–1, 253–4), a vow that is partly fulfilled at the end of the play when Giovanni kills Annabella.

Nevertheless, the scene also suggests the irresistibility of their love and encourages an audience to be sympathetic towards it. For example, there is here none of the moral repugnance or condemnation of incest that Giovanni encountered when he spoke to the Friar. Annabella points out that he is her brother but then immediately succumbs because his passion exactly mirrors her own. Her response seems to reinforce Giovanni's assumption that they are essentially made for each other, that it would be a sin 'To share one beauty to a double soul' (line 233). This notion reflects the **Neoplatonic** idea that love unites souls that were once a complete whole but have since been painfully divided. It also suggests that Giovanni perceives himself and Annabella as sharing the same physical beauty and this may be reinforced if actors are cast who strongly resemble one another.

What is perhaps chiefly notable in this scene is the way in which the lovers' language and actions mirror one another, suggesting compatibility, intimacy and love. Lines 207–8, where Giovanni persuades Annabella that he really does love her incestuously, consist of extremely brief, even one-word, utterances divided between the two speakers. This technique of the **split-line** quickens the pace of the dialogue and builds suspense. There is a famous example in Shakespeare's *King John* (1595) in which a murder is plotted:

KING JOHN   Death.

HUBERT   My lord.

KING JOHN   A grave.

HUBERT   He shall not live.

KING JOHN   Enough. (III.3.66)

However, the use of split-lines could also create a less sinister, more romantic intimacy, suggesting how well suited two people are who generate a line of verse together, and acting as a prelude to a more erotic coupling. From Annabella's confession onwards, the couple are paralleled through their language and their actions. They repeat the same vows; they both kneel facing one another; they kiss, and they exit the stage for bed.

CHECK THE BOOK
Annabella's guilty admission that she is too easily persuaded to return Giovanni's love: 'Thou hast won/ The field and never fought' (lines 239–40), strongly recalls Juliet's similar doubts expressed in the balcony scene in *Romeo and Juliet*: 'I should have been more strange [reserved] I must confess' (II.1.144).

QUESTION
The idea of Neoplatonic love was extremely popular at the Caroline court (see **Literary background: Caroline drama**). Do you think that Ford is mocking such language by placing it in the mouth of an incestuous lover?

CHECK THE BOOK

Shakespeare's **Sonnet** XX suggests that the ideal male companion is another man, one as beautiful as a woman but with a man's ability to be both loving and faithful.

CONTEXT

Images of saints were often condemned for inspiring idolatry. Among radical Protestants there was a suspicion of art's affective power in general. In John Webster's *The White Devil* (1612), Isabella's idolatrous act of kissing a painting of her husband is punished with her death.

TEXT 2 – IV.3.106–46 (PP. 132–4)

From 'O Vasques' to 'to your chamber.'

On discovering that Annabella is pregnant, Soranzo has raged at her and even threatened to kill her. In this passage, he follows Vasques' advice by turning his anger into grief but reveals in the process how conflicted he feels about his love for Annabella.

Soranzo's anguished cry 'O Vasques, Vasques' (line 106) is part of the performance of grief required of him. Rather than address Annabella directly, in lines 106–8 Soranzo talks about her to his servant, making her a witness to his sufferings on her behalf. There is also something psychologically convincing about the way in which Soranzo turns to Vasques, not only a loyal servant and confidant but a man. Men's affections were generally considered more constant than those of woman and Soranzo's reliance upon the masculine now expresses his sense of betrayal by the feminine.

Soranzo refers again and again to the deceptiveness of Annabella's beauty, often by means of the oxymoron: she is a 'fair, wicked woman' (line 109) – 'fair' usually meant both beautiful and virtuous. Similarly, Annabella's face is described contemptuously as a 'piece of flesh' (line 106), recalling the biblical warnings against the perils of 'the flesh' i.e. lust, and the way in which all mortal bodies (and their pleasures) will inevitably decay. At the same time, she is also identified with the divine: Soranzo suggests that he would forego all other worldly pleasures (including other women), wishing to live with no other 'saint but thee' (line 111).

Soranzo recognises that this displacement of God by a mortal creature is a form of idolatry, asking Annabella: 'didst not think that in my heart/ I did too superstitiously adore thee?' (lines 118–19). At the same time, he is willing to defend this love, arguing that rather than being fixated on her superficial beauty he loved her for herself. Specifically, it was not the 'picture' (line 125) of Annabella's beauty but her heart that he doted on (perhaps meaning her capacity for love, her essential being), and her virtues. Nevertheless, the isolation of a 'part' (line 127) that he loves anticipates Giovanni's cutting out of the heart at the end of the play. Indeed, this passage repeatedly identifies love with possessiveness and being possessed. Both Giovanni and Soranzo think of Annabella as a receptacle for something precious – their love, their trust, their sense of self – but this image becomes increasingly disturbing. Soranzo describes how he had 'laid up/ The treasure of my heart!' (lines 107–8) in Annabella's beauty; Giovanni holds up Annabella's heart and insists ''Tis a heart … in which mine is entombed' (V.6.26–7). The passionate love that both men feel for Annabella becomes destructive and claustrophobic, and they have violent fantasies about liberating themselves (and their hearts) from its power.

Throughout the passage, Soranzo's emotional state is **ambiguous**. He has declared his intention to imitate grief so as to deceive Annabella and to throw her off her guard, but we cannot be sure where the distinction between acting and 'real' emotion lies. Vasques suggests that Soranzo is weeping as he speaks (line 130) and that he might elicit the same response from the spectator. Annabella also insists that this is a moving performance: 'These words wound deeper than your sword could do' (line 129) and seems ready to repent. Ford may have taken his inspiration for this scene from *Hamlet*, a play in which we cannot always be sure whether the **protagonist** is mad or is merely pretending to be mad. More specifically, in the famous closet scene of Act III Scene 3, Hamlet switches between violence and a heart-rending performance of grief when he accuses his mother, Gertrude, of adultery. He terrifies her by threatening her with his dagger and then makes her (and perhaps himself) weep out of guilt. Ford suggests the same passionate conflict between hatred and love, the desire for revenge and repentance, in *'Tis Pity*. Like Hamlet, Soranzo ends this scene playing the role of religious confessor. His promise that if Annabella repents then he will offer her forgiveness: 'here I remit/ All former faults, and take thee to my bosom' (lines 138–9) makes him a double not only for the Friar but for a loving and merciful Christ. Moreover, Soranzo's emphasis on the divinity of the name 'husband' also reminds us of the way in which patriarchal authority in early modern England was endorsed by the teachings of the Bible. Soranzo may not be that much older than Annabella but his repeated emphasis on her youth and the ease with which she has been tempted into folly implies the necessity for a woman to be controlled by a male authority figure. This also links Annabella to the biblical figure of Eve who was tempted by the serpent and thus brought about the fall of man (see **Contemporary perspectives: A feminist reading**). The fact that Annabella kneels before Soranzo reflects her submission to his

> **CONTEXT**
>
> Husbands and wives would have been familiar with biblical passages, read aloud in church every day, such as *Ephesians* 5:22–3: 'Wives, submit yourselves unto your husbands, as unto the Lord. For the husband is the head of the wife, even as Christ is the head of the church'.

authority as husband and perhaps her status as a 'fallen Eve'. It also echoes her kneeling before the Friar in III.6. More ominously, however, it emphasises that the mutual love and sympathy that Annabella once had with Giovanni (where he also kneeled) has been lost, replaced by an inevitably unequal and repressive marriage, and by a love affair which is becoming increasingly destructive. Ultimately, what Soranzo and Giovanni both seek from Annabella is not repentance and reformation but revenge.

TEXT 3 – V.6.10–38 (PP. 157–8)

From 'Enter Giovanni' to 'your son.'

In this extract, Giovanni interrupts the birthday feast, with a dagger on which a heart is impaled. He tries to explain to the horrified spectators what he has done, attempting to justify it as an act of courage, defiance, even love.

Giovanni's first words describe his own appearance as being 'trimmed in reeking blood' (line 10). 'Trimmed' means covered but it also suggests adornment. The notion that blood should be an attractive decoration immediately suggests Giovanni's disordered values. His triumphant self-display continues in the subsequent lines: 'proud in the spoil/ Of love and vengeance' (lines 11–12). This is contradictory. On the one hand, it suggests that Giovanni has conquered love and vengeance by killing Annabella and spoiling Soranzo's planned revenge. However, if we interpret 'spoil' as meaning 'plunder', then Giovanni seems to be imagining himself as the **personification** of Love and Vengeance combined, with blood as a physical manifestation of his triumph, a kind of trophy.

Having caused a sensation by his mere appearance, Giovanni goes on to boast of the unseen violence he has performed. He takes the spectators' response of fear and loathing as an indication of their inferiority to himself, rather than a sign of their humanity:

CONTEXT

Giovanni may be likening himself to Cupid here who was often depicted carrying a bleeding and impaled heart to symbolise the triumph of love.

If your misgiving hearts
Shrink at an idle sight, what bloodless fear
Of coward passion would have seized your senses,
Had you beheld the rape of life and beauty
Which I have acted. (lines 16–20)

This speech is full of **wordplay**. 'Idle' emphasises that neither the audience on stage nor the audience in the theatre has seen the actual violence of Annabella's death, only a symbolic representation of it. This representation is inevitably less emotionally affecting than the 'real thing', and therefore 'idle' is used to mean passive, comparatively unstimulating. However, 'idle' is also a **homonym** for 'idol' and idolatry has been a characteristic of Giovanni's love throughout the play – he is displaying the heart that he has idolised.

Further **puns** are focused on the words 'heart' and 'blood' (see also **Language: Words and images**). Both were associated with love/lust but also with courage. Thus, Giovanni taunts his spectators that he possesses 'heart' (courage) as symbolised by his holding a heart (line 9), where they are fearful, as expressed by their 'misgiving hearts' (line 16). Similarly, the fact that he appears covered in blood contrasts with the 'bloodless fear' (line 17) that would have struck his audience if they had seen what he has seen. Finally, the use of the word 'rape' (line 18) is striking to describe Giovanni's violence against Annabella. 'Rape' at this time was a more general term that could mean abduction or theft. Giovanni has not only stolen Annabella's heart from her body, he has also stolen from her beauty and life. Yet the sexual sense of 'rape' is also implied, with Giovanni apparently taking erotic pleasure in stabbing Annabella and using this as a means to assert his power over her.

Throughout this passage, Giovanni's attempts to justify what he has done implicitly condemn him, a fact to which he seems quite unconscious. In line 21, he describes 'the glory of my deed'. 'Glory' was often associated with light, but here the 'glory of my deed/ Darkened the midday sun'. A solar eclipse was understood at this time as a portent of evil or as a sign of earth's shame at some terrible crime. According to the Gospels, the earth fell dark after the crucifixion of Christ. In Shakespeare's *Macbeth*, the murder of

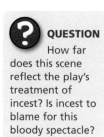

QUESTION
How far does this scene reflect the play's treatment of incest? Is incest to blame for this bloody spectacle?

the king, also casts a literal darkness upon the kingdom. Similarly, in lines 31–3, Giovanni describes how

> This dagger's point ploughed up
> Her fruitful womb, and left to me the fame
> Of a most glorious executioner.

CHECK THE BOOK

In Shakespeare's *Measure for Measure* (1603), a former pimp called Pompey is ordered to work alongside Abhorson, the executioner. Abhorson complains that this will discredit his profession but the Provost disagrees: 'you weigh equally; a feather will turn the scale' (IV.2.22–3).

For Ford's audience, even more so than for us, the phrase 'glorious executioner' would have seemed an **oxymoron**, for to be an executioner was one of the most miserable and ignoble jobs possible in early modern England, certainly not a guarantor of 'fame'. We might also note how Giovanni confuses the act of destruction with the act of creation. The image of ploughing up Annabella's 'fruitful womb' is erotic and agricultural, likening the womb to a field that needs to be prepared for sowing. But as the onstage spectators will shortly discover, Annabella was already pregnant when she died. The further act of ploughing this field (and with a dagger) thus proves destructive, killing Annabella and Giovanni's unborn child. Indeed, we may wonder whether Giovanni has performed a deliberate act of abortion.

Finally, Giovanni promises that he will prove to Florio 'how much I have deserved to be your son' (line 38). Again, this has a double meaning. Giovanni insists that his acts are noble and therefore worthy of Florio, but also by having sex with his sister and, indeed, improvising a marriage with her, he has effectively become Florio's son-in-law as well as his son. Once again, Giovanni entirely misjudges his audience's reactions – Florio will die of grief and shame when he hears what Giovanni has done. Nevertheless, there may be a further connection here between patriarchal authority as represented by Giovanni and that exercised by Florio and Soranzo. Throughout the play, Annabella is viewed as the possession of one man or another. Competition between these men literally tears her apart. Moreover, the monetary value Giovanni places upon her when he describes her body as 'a much richer mine than gold or stone' (line 25) reminds us that Annabella's marriage negotiations have centred on her fiscal value, in particular the value attached to that 'jewel' her virginity. Although Giovanni's actions in this final scene are extreme and horrifying, they are not simply attributable to his deviant nature but may reflect a distorted version of the values of his father and his society. The occurance today of murders perpetuated by a man against his wife and his children, often in response to the wife's infidelity or remarriage, reminds us that there is not such a distance between our ideas of masculine authority, family and gender politics and those of Ford's society. The drive to possess another person remains potentially destructive.

QUESTION
Given that *'Tis Pity She's a Whore* so often makes a connection between love and death, should we classify it as a love tragedy rather than a revenge tragedy? Could it be both?

CRITICAL APPROACHES

CHARACTERISATION

GIOVANNI

Giovanni (whose name in Italian means 'young man') is described at the beginning of the play as a youth already in decline. His tutor, Friar Bonaventura, mournfully recalls: 'How did the university applaud/ Thy government, behaviour, learning, speech,/ Sweetness, and all that could make up a man!' (I.1.50–2). His own sister, Annabella, does not recognise him: 'Sure 'tis not he: this is some woeful thing/ Wrapped up in grief, some shadow of a man' (I.2.132–3).

Ford's original audience would have found at least two explanations for this deterioration. Firstly, Giovanni has recently been a student at the University of Bologna. His brooding melancholy, his self-isolation, and his asceticism were all part of the stereotype of the student in early modern England. Hence, Florio pleads with him to 'forsake/ This over-bookish humour' (II.6.118–19). Yet Ford's audience would also have recognised Giovanni's tears, sighs and shunning of company as the behaviour of the unsatisfied or unrequited lover. In *Romeo and Juliet*, Romeo's father seeks his son, only to be told that he has withdrawn into a grove of sycamore, a tree whose name identified it with the melancholic lover ('sick-amour'). There he has been seen: 'With tears augmenting the fresh morning's dew,/ Adding to clouds more clouds with his deep sighs' (I.1.129–30).

What distinguishes Giovanni's from the usual melancholy of the student and the lover is incest – the fact that he desires his own sister – which places tremendous strain on his already over-wrought intellect and emotions.

At the beginning of the play it is clear that he has lost neither his ability to construct an argument nor his eloquence. Yet by defending incest, a practice strictly against the laws of man and of God, his reason directly undermines his faith, leading the Friar to accuse him of blasphemy and atheism (see **Themes: Fate and damnation**). Subsequently, Giovanni is established as a man who dangerously misapplies both his intellect and his eloquence in order to satisfy his lust. Not only does he invent arguments to justify incest, he also asserts that sex outside marriage and a woman's loss of chastity are not serious matters (II.1.9–12). There would have been no question for Ford's audience that Giovanni was wrong on both counts.

Equally, it might be argued that Giovanni suffers more than the stereotypical lover, both because incest's satisfaction is so dangerous – 'I see my ruin, certain' (I.2.142) – but also because, paradoxically, his desire for his sister feels more compelling and more inevitable than any other kind of heterosexual love: 'Nearness in birth or blood doth but persuade a nearness in affection' (I.2.234–5). Moreover, just as incestuous desire seems to warp Giovanni's intellectual prowess so that he begins to force arguments that are illogical, it might also be said to distort his capacity to love. In the course of the play he becomes increasingly jealous, possessive and paranoid. By the end of the play, he is calling murder an act of love (see **Literary background: Ford and Shakespeare**).

The defence and then practice of incest that separates Giovanni ideologically from the rest of society is represented on stage by his physical isolation. He begins the play in private discussion with the Friar and ends this first scene promising to lock himself in his chamber in order to weep, pray and fast (I.1.69–70). He is rarely to be found in any of the lively, bustling scenes of the play. When forced to attend his sister's wedding-feast, he does so ungraciously, refusing to toast the couple's health (IV.1.27), and he is frequently placed in the position of observer, uttering asides that only the audience can hear. This isolation is important not only because it represents the way in which Giovanni's thinking alienates him from society but because it might partly explain his feelings for Annabella. Perhaps Giovanni actually prefers a secret, incestuous love because it corresponds to his habits of seclusion and introspection. Rather than practise exogamy – which means to marry someone from a different family, tribe or clan (literally marrying out) – he turns inwards, looking to the womb that gave

CHECK THE BOOK

Robert Burton devoted a whole text to the description and discussion of melancholic personalities. See *The Anatomy of Melancholy* (1621).

him birth to provide him with a lover (see also **Contemporary perspectives: A cultural materialist reading**).

Nevertheless, Giovanni's jealousy and possessiveness in the course of the play destroy his capacity for love and for any kind of empathy. His erratic and violent behaviour in the later scenes has often been interpreted as a sign of insanity. For a seventeenth-century audience, madness was understood to be an expression of God's wrath and a punishment for sin (I.1.24). It could also be explained as an effect of excessive melancholy or frustrated love. But again, madness relates to and reinforces Giovanni's isolation. In the final scene, he seems emotionally disconnected from everyone else in the play. He is surprised by his father's horror at the revelation of incest and fails to show either remorse or grief when Florio suddenly dies. One of the behaviours believed to be a symptom of madness in the seventeenth century was an inability to recognise family members. This applies metaphorically not only to Giovanni's relationship to Florio but also to his sister/lover, Annabella, and even to his unborn child. In this way, Giovanni and Annabella's experiences of incestuous love are strikingly divergent. She retains an understanding of conventional morality and of familial duty, declaring at the end that Giovanni has been 'unkind' (V.5.93) to kill her, meaning that he has acted in defiance of what is owed to one's kin. She retains the capacity for guilt, love and compassion where Giovanni becomes increasingly amoral and self-absorbed. His fall, from a brilliant and promising young man to a suicidal killer, makes him the tragic hero of his own story, but the villain of Annabella's.

ANNABELLA

What seems to strike every character in the play about Annabella is her beauty. Giovanni describes it as greater 'than art can counterfeit or nature frame' (I.2.201) and blames it for 'enflaming' him with desire: 'Such lips would tempt a saint; such hands as these/ Would make an anchorite lascivious' (197–8). Soranzo argues that the poet, Sannazaro, would have praised Annabella and her 'diviner cheeks' (II.2.16–17). She is called 'Fair Annabella' (II.3.39) and 'Fair gentlewoman' (II.6.6) by Donado and Grimaldi. Yet there is more to Annabella than her physical attractions.

CONTEXT

In his French adaptation of the play in 1894, Maurice Maeterlinck emphasised the importance he saw in Annabella's role by naming the play after her alone.

Where isolation and secrecy seem to suit Giovanni, Annabella is a much more gregarious character who is often remarkably candid. She professes to have found it difficult to keep her love for Giovanni secret, weeping 'not so much for that I loved, as that/ I durst not say I loved, nor scarcely think it' (I.2.245–6). She refuses to trifle with the feelings of Bergetto, telling Donado frankly that she will not marry his nephew (II.4.54). When Soranzo discovers her pregnancy, Annabella seems relieved at no longer having to keep her secret. Throughout the play, she is forced to practise guile and hypocrisy but it does not come easily to her.

Of the two incestuous lovers, it is notable that Annabella is the only one whom the Friar seems to have some hopes of saving. She has two repentance scenes (Act III Scene 6 and Act V Scene 1) in which the Friar's dire warnings of damnation and her own belief that incest and adultery are sins make her repent her love for Giovanni. Yet Annabella is not entirely consistent. Despite her repentance before marriage, Giovanni tells us that she continues to sleep with him after it. She is defiant and then placatory towards Soranzo in Act IV Scene 3, but her loyalty remains with Giovanni. The struggle between sin and virtue, transgression and conformity is most clearly dramatised through Annabella, but her 'real' feelings are difficult for an audience to judge.

Ultimately, Ford limits Annabella's capacity for heroism. In Act IV Scene 3, she is ready to die to protect her lover's identity but she seems to succumb to fear towards the end of the play. She dies, not through an act of suicide to save her brother, but by his hand, as a victim of his revenge. In the final scene, she is reduced to a mere piece of flesh – her body remaining offstage. Nor is it entirely clear what happens to this body. Some critics have wondered whether the Cardinal's command that 'This woman, chief in these effects ... be burnt to ashes' (V.6.132, 135) refers to Putana or to Annabella. Above all, the play's final line, ''Tis pity she's a whore' (V.6.159) hardly seems an appropriate epitaph for this once complex and sympathetic character. Yet perhaps this was Ford's intention. We might wonder whether, by using this word to describe Annabella, he was commenting on the way in which the prevailing cultural stereotypes of women were not only inadequate to describe them but justified their oppression and even encouraged violence against

CHECK THE BOOK

In Webster's *The White Devil*, one of the central female characters, Vittoria, is described as a 'whore', but she responds scornfully: 'Ha? Whore, what's that?' (III.2.78). When the Cardinal explains, describing the whore as 'sweetmeats which rot the eater . . . poisoned perfumes . . . the true material fire of hell' (81–2, 86), Vittoria insists that 'This character scapes me' (line 102).

them (see **Contemporary perspectives: A feminist reading**). Certainly, Annabella remains the emotional centre of the play, the focus around which all the plots move, and her role has invariably overshadowed that of Giovanni in performance.

FRIAR BONAVENTURA

Ford's Friar is clearly borrowed from Shakespeare's *Romeo and Juliet*. Like Friar Lawrence, he is a confidant to the male protagonist, offers philosophical guidance, arranges a wedding and ultimately fails to save the lovers from tragedy, taking flight to avoid disaster himself. Perhaps the most significant alteration Ford has made is to the Friar's name, thus clarifying his religious affiliation and his function in society.

Bonaventura was a thirteenth-century monk and philosopher who was made a saint by the Catholic Church in 1482. He was a member of the Franciscan order, followers of St Francis of Assisi, who lived among the lay community. They cared for the sick, preached and depended on alms (charity) for their existence. Bonaventura was also a famous teacher who left Italy to take up a position in the University of Paris, another connection with Ford's Friar who teaches at the University of Bologna.

 **CHECK THE BOOK**

Marlowe's play *The Jew of Malta* (1590) contains a thoroughly scurrilous depiction of monks and nuns. When the beautiful Abigail, who has joined a convent, dies, her last words are 'I die a Christian!' The Friar on stage with her at the time adds 'Ay, and a virgin too; that grieves me most' (III.6.40–1). There may be a similar undertone of lust to the Cardinal's last lines about Annabella.

By giving his Friar this illustrious background, Ford has pre-empted, or at least complicated, the hostile reactions that such a figure tended to provoke on stage. Friars were obviously members of the Catholic Church and thus objects of suspicion and even hatred for English Protestants. As part of the Reformation in England, monasteries had been closed down across England, releasing their inhabitants into the secular world. The reason for this was mainly financial (Henry VIII needed the wealth owned by the monasteries) but it was more often justified as a way of punishing the vices associated with these religious communities. Monks were habitually accused of breaking their vow of chastity (with nuns and with one another), of greed and political ambition.

By contrast, the Friar in *'Tis Pity She's a Whore* appears virtuous and sincere. He cannot be accused of pursuing his own interests (unlike Friar Lawrence in *Romeo and Juliet*) and he takes no pleasure in the idea of the lovers' sexual transgression. At worst, the Friar is exposed as being ineffectual and a coward. His philosophy makes no impression on Giovanni, and he has only partial success with Annabella by terrifying her with vivid scenes of hell. Rather than stay until the end of the play in order to try to prevent the tragedy, he escapes, abandoning the couple to their fate.

PUTANA

Putana is clearly modelled on the figure of the Nurse in Shakespeare's *Romeo and Juliet*. As in that play, she serves as the confidante of her young female charge, has a more liberal attitude towards sex than the other parental figures, and provides moments of comic relief. Yet Ford's character is also morally darker, incurring sharper condemnation at the end of the play. In the Italian dictionary that Ford consulted, 'puttanna' meant 'whore'. The fact that this character is elsewhere described as Annabella's 'guardian' and 'tut'ress' is, then, rather ominous. Most shocking is Putana's complacency about incest. She tells Annabella: 'Fear nothing, sweetheart, what though he be your brother? Your brother's a man I hope, and I say still, if a young wench feel the fit upon her, let her take anybody, father or brother, all is one' (II.1.43–5).

Putana seems to be genuinely loyal to Annabella. Yet she is also keen to promote her own financial interests. In Act I Scene 2, she suggests that she would accept a bribe to leave Annabella alone with one of her suitors (line 170). In Act II Scene 6, she takes money from Donado to persuade Annabella to love Bergetto (lines 14–22). This all seems harmless enough, until Act IV Scene 3 when she betrays Annabella and Giovanni's secret to Vasques – a catastrophic error of judgement. Partly, Putana acts out of sympathy for her mistress and out of her own distress, for she too has suffered at the hands of an angry, violent Soranzo. She is naive, perhaps, to believe that revealing Giovanni's identity will actually help Annabella, but then Vasques is very persuasive. What is less appealing is the hint that once again Putana is willing to be bought, revealing the secret in return for 'everlasting love and preferment' (line 202).

Putana's blinding is far in excess of her crime, but it reflects that crime as the play perceives it. Her eyes are put out in recognition that she has seen and overseen something that she should not have done. Moreover, the Cardinal's insistence that her body be 'ta'en/ Out of the city . . . There to be burnt to ashes' (V.6.133–5)

> **CONTEXT**
>
> In myth and literature, blindness has often been associated with sexual crime. In Sophocles' tragedy, *Oedipus Rex*, the king, who has committed incest with his own mother, blinds himself. In Shakespeare's *King Lear*, the blinding of Gloucester is partly understood as a punishment for adultery and for fathering an illegitimate child.

acknowledges the anti-social nature of her actions. It aligns her with the religious heretic and the witch for whom burning was a standard punishment. This terrible fate suffered by an essentially comic figure demonstrates just how far from the more liberal attitude towards incest *'Tis Pity She's a Whore* seems to have come. It also suggests how easily women in the play become scapegoats (see **Contemporary perspectives: A feminist reading**).

SORANZO

Playboy, poet and adulterer, Lord Soranzo moves through Parma society with the aristocrat's confidence and sense of entitlement. Like Giovanni, he has little patience with conventional morality. He is happy to sleep with the married Hippolita and then to abandon her, despite his promises of marriage. When she condemns his faithlessness, he finds morality a useful form of self-justification: 'The vows I made, if you remember well,/ Were wicked and unlawful,/ 'twere more sin/ To keep them than to break them' (II.2.85–7).

CONTEXT

Servants in seventeenth-century England were often included in their master's wills as a form of bequest, along with money and property.

Yet Soranzo is not as invulnerable as he appears. In the course of the play, the threats against his life increase in number: Grimaldi, Richardetto, Hippolita and Giovanni all want him dead. Moreover, the fact that he survives as long as he does is really nothing to do with Soranzo himself, but is attributable to the cunning of Vasques, a servant he seems to have inherited from his father. It is striking that Soranzo needs Vasques to help him take his revenge. Apparently, he has the violent temperament but he lacks the necessary self-control, being ready to kill Annabella in Act IV though this would defeat his hopes of discovering the identity of her lover. Equally, he is not as resolute as Vasques could wish. He seems susceptible to pity in Act V Scene 2, and has to be goaded by Vasques into remembering the wrongs Annabella has done him.

Critics have sometimes argued that Soranzo is Giovanni's opposite. Where the latter is infatuated with Annabella, to the point of obsession, Soranzo is characterised by the fickleness of his desire. Yet, in the course of the play, he arguably reveals a deeper feeling for Annabella. He is stricken with grief when she refuses to marry him and suddenly falls ill; he is ecstatic when she changes her mind. Later, discovering her betrayal, he weeps tears that may be genuine. Though his plan to kill Annabella seems to contradict the notion that he loves her, Soranzo strongly resembles another lover-turned-killer, Shakespeare's Othello. Unlike Othello, however, he remains a fairly marginal character in the play. He is consistently upstaged by Giovanni, both as a lover and as a revenger, and he dies before his revenge is achieved. Once again, he must rely on his faithful servant, Vasques, to finish what he has left undone.

VASQUES

Vasques is an outsider – he is Spanish not Italian, and he is of lower social status than the other characters (with the exception of Putana and Poggio) – yet he occupies a central role in the play.

Vasques is initially defined by an unflinching devotion to his master, Soranzo. He risks his own life to fight Soranzo's rival, Grimaldi, and he tries to shield the former from Hippolita, fearing otherwise that he will be accused of a 'neglect of duty and service' (II.2.20). Although the terms 'servile', 'slavish', and 'peasant' were all insults in seventeenth-century England, suggesting the shame of being subordinate, the notion of service was also held in high esteem. As the writer, Nicholas Ling, expressed it, in a tract called *Politeuphia or Wit's Commonwealth* (1597): 'To serve or obey well, is a great vertue . . . Nature, and the lawes which preserve nature, bind men that will be servants, to strict obedience.' Whether or not Soranzo deserves such loyalty remains to be seen. Indeed, Hippolita plays on Vasques' doubts, arguing that Soranzo will prove as ungrateful to his servant as he has proved to his mistress (II.2.126–8). The fact that Vasques seems to be relatively old – he expresses the wish 'to live in these my old years with rest and security' (II.2.145–6) – makes this anxiety more acute. At a time when there was no form of pension for the elderly servant, once cast off by his master he could be left in abject poverty. If, on the other hand, Vasques marries Hippolita, he will become the master himself, rising considerably in wealth and social status.

For all the audience knows, then, Vasques has indeed betrayed Soranzo by conspiring with Hippolita. It is only after he foils Hippolita's plan by giving the cup of poison to her rather than to Soranzo that we are assured of his unstinting loyalty. As he tells the assembled wedding guests in Act IV Scene 1, he has merely played the role of Hippolita's ally in order to double-cross her and protect

CONTEXT

Othello is another jealous husband who decides to kill his wife at the instigation of his subordinate, Iago. In Shakespeare's play, however, the wife is innocent and they are all victims of Iago's duplicity. For a more detailed discussion of *'Tis Pity*'s debt to *Othello* see **Literary background: Ford and Shakespeare**.

 CHECK THE BOOK

In Richard Brome's play, *The English Moor; or the Mock-Marriage* (1637–8), an old servant called Arnold finds himself in dire financial need after being cast off by two masters. His only alternatives are begging or stealing.

VASQUES continued

CHECK THE BOOK

Ben Jonson's comedies *Every Man in his Humour* (1598) and *Volpone* both feature servants who disguise themselves and perform elaborate tricks in order to benefit their masters, whilst also taking pleasure in the deception for its own sake.

CONTEXT

In classical mythology, an Amazon was a woman who chose to live in a society of women, using men only to reproduce. Amazons were famous for their fierce fighting ability. They were often depicted as having cut off a breast in order to facilitate the use of a bow and arrow. They were also notorious for their cruelty to their male children whom they killed or maimed.

his master. For this, he wins Soranzo's gratitude and, perhaps, his own future security: 'Vasques, I know thee now a trusty servant and never will forget thee' (IV.1.100–1). Faithful service (even though it involves murder) has proved its own reward.

There is certainly potential for Vasques to be a sympathetic character. His admirable cleverness on his master's behalf identifies him with the cunning slave of Ancient Roman comedies by Plautus and Terence, imitated in the seventeenth century by Ben Jonson and Thomas Middleton. Yet alongside these traits, Vasques also shows a disturbing taste for violence and a vicious sense of humour. He is full of glee to discover that Annabella's lover is her brother, Giovanni, and he takes sadistic delight in the persuasion and then punishment of Putana. In fact, this seems to be Vasques' preferred method of dealing with women – feigning sympathy and then betraying them – as we see with Hippolita and, to a lesser extent, Annabella. With men, he is much more direct and straightforward, wounding Giovanni himself before calling in the *banditti* to finish the job.

To the end of the play, Vasques remains an enigma. There seems insufficient motivation for his extreme loyalty to Soranzo, but his explanation that he wanted to surpass an Italian in revenge (V.6.145–6) is equally unconvincing. His curious blend of villainy and virtue, transgression and obedience, is punished with exile at the end of the play. He will be sent back to Spain, without a master. Yet rather than express any fears for his future, Vasques implies that this is a kind of freedom: 'This strange task being ended, I have paid the duty to the son which I have vowed to the father' (V.6.110–12). Possibly Ford was remembering Plautus' *Menaechmi* or *Rudens*, comedies in which the slave won his freedom through faithful service. Yet this is a **tragedy** and the fact that Vasques-the-murderer lives creates a sense of injustice and unease at the end of the play.

HIPPOLITA

Hippolita's name alone would have suggested to Ford's audience that she was a woman driven by desire and capable of violence. In classical mythology, Hippolita is an Amazon queen defeated in battle by Theseus, and an adulteress who takes revenge on a young man who refuses her advances.

From the beginning of *'Tis Pity She's a Whore*, Ford's Hippolita is a character defined by passion. She is furious with Soranzo for seducing her, for encouraging her to 'kill' her husband, and for breaking his promise of marriage. Rather than express guilt or remorse, however, Soranzo blames Hippolita for the lust that allowed her to be seduced and for being now 'too violent' in her speech (II.2.51). When Hippolita cannot find satisfaction in verbally abusing Soranzo, she turns to physical violence, recalling the female revenger of Jacobean tragedy who murdered in order to fulfill her sexual desires, or who took revenge when her passion was thwarted. Such women were invariably punished by death at the end of the play, just as Richardetto points the moral in Hippolita's death: 'Here's the end/ Of lust and pride' (IV.1.98–9).

CHECK THE BOOK

Examples of female revengers in Jacobean tragedy include Livia and Bianca in Middleton's *Women Beware Women* and the eponymous heroine of Marston, Barksted and Machin's *The Insatiate Countess* (1610).

Yet, there is much about Hippolita's character that belies this simple moral. For example, although she blames herself for having caused her husband's death, in fact she simply encouraged Richardetto to undertake a dangerous journey in order to bring back Philotis. She is obviously guilty of wishing her husband dead but she is hardly a murderess at this stage. Similarly, although she is accused of lust by Soranzo, Vasques and Richardetto ('Thy wanton aunt in her lascivious riots . . .' [II.3.7]), Hippolita does not understand her actions as lustful. She suggests rather that it was the power of Soranzo's rhetoric that won her heart and that she was moved by pity not desire (II.2.35–7). Here, Ford turns to a different kind of literature to create an alternative perspective on Hippolita. In her first speech, she blames Soranzo: 'Look, perjured man, on her/ Whom thou and thy distracted lust have wronged' (II.2.26–7). This identifies her with the speaker of the Complaint, a poetic form, popular in the 1590s, in which a female character expressed her suffering on being seduced and then abandoned by her male lover. Like Hippolita, the speaker of the Complaint would often single out the seducer's rhetorical skill, blaming this for her submission.

CHECK THE BOOK

Some famous Complaint poems are Samuel Daniel's *The Complaint of Rosamond* (1592) and Shakespeare's *A Lover's Complaint* (c.1600), both of which were written to accompany a **sonnet sequence**. In this way, the desiring male voice of the sonnet is followed by the mournful female voice of the Complaint.

Hippolita is then both villain and victim – a contradiction that is never resolved by Ford's tragedy (see **Contemporary perspectives: A feminist reading**). She is intriguing not only in her own right but for the way in which she sets up the ambiguity surrounding Annabella, the eponymous 'whore' of the play.

CHECK THE BOOK
Like Bergetto, the Ward in *Women Beware Women* woos a woman far superior to him and is accepted because she is already pregnant by her uncle (another link with *'Tis Pity*). However, the Ward is lascivious and misogynist; he has far less charm than Bergetto.

BERGETTO

The character of Bergetto seems intended to suggest how limited are Annabella's possibilities for happiness in marriage and therefore how attractive her brother, Giovanni, looks by comparison. Bergetto is one of a trio of unsuitable suitors: there is Grimaldi, the violent soldier; Soranzo, the adulterer and libertine; and finally Bergetto, an object of scorn for his stupidity and childish pleasures, probably based on the Ward in Middleton's tragedy, *Women Beware Women* (1621).

Anyone can see – including Florio who calls him 'the fool' – that Bergetto is no match for Annabella (II.6.120). The fact that the negotiations go as far as they do is a reflection of the financial motives behind the courtship (see **Themes: Marriage**), and of the friendship between the two legal guardians, Florio and Donado.

At the same time, Bergetto is also an important source of comedy in the play. He has no interest in wooing Annabella and when he does attempt to flatter her he does it ineptly, causing offence rather than stirring affection. His uncle frequently despairs of him:

> Wilt thou be a fool still? . . . You have more mind of a puppet-play than on the business I told ye. Why, thou great baby, wilt thou . . . make thyself a May-game to all the world? (I.3.44–7)

But if Bergetto's naivety makes him a source of mockery, it also contrasts with those around him who are more sophisticated and more treacherous. His inability to flatter Annabella partly reflects the fact that he does not care for her. When he falls for Philotis, it is a relationship based on affection (Philotis' name means 'Affection' or 'Love' in Greek) and there is something touching in their heartfelt exchange of gifts and kisses that makes Annabella's courtship and marriage to Soranzo look even more contrived. Bergetto's desire to escape to the fairground, literally evading enclosure in his uncle's house (II.4.41–2), implies the repressive atmosphere of Parma. It also suggests the possibility of a form of pleasure that does not involve either illicit sex or violence. Bergetto's accidental death is genuinely shocking. It hints that there

QUESTION
Can you see any parallels between the situation of Bergetto in the play and that of Annabella?

is no place for innocence in the world of the play and seems to set it more firmly on course towards its tragic conclusion.

FLORIO, DONADO, RICHARDETTO AND PHILOTIS

Florio is a considerably more sympathetic version of Capulet in Shakespeare's *Romeo and Juliet*. Both fathers begin their respective plays by insisting that they want their daughters to marry for love. Capulet, however, turns violently against his daughter when she refuses to marry Paris. By contrast, Florio urges the marriage with Soranzo but never becomes a tyrannical father since Annabella's pregnancy makes the match expedient to her (see **Literary background: Ford and Shakespeare**). In general, Florio keeps his financial and social ambitions for Annabella in check and gives her considerable freedom to make her own choice of husband. It might be argued that his desire to marry Annabella off (with all its benefits) blinds him to the illicit affair she is conducting with her brother but this hardly seems fair. No one else, including Annabella's own husband, has any suspicion. Indeed, the revelation of incest is so shocking that it has the power to kill. Exactly what emotion it is that stops Florio's heart – whether grief at Annabella's death or shame for her and Giovanni's sin or both – is left uncertain.

Donado is a kind of surrogate father for Bergetto, of a similar cast to Florio. He blusters more than Florio, threatening his nephew with physical punishment if he will not stay in the house (II.4.42), and repeatedly upbraiding him for his foolishness, to his face and in **asides** to the audience. He is often acutely embarrassed by Bergetto, hence the fact that he so often intervenes in the courtship, for example writing the letter to Annabella himself (II.4.30). Yet Donado is also greatly moved by Bergetto's death. He appears on stage weeping and the rebuke that was so often applied to his nephew, that he 'show[ed] [him]self a child' (III.9.1) is now applied to him. Having failed to get justice for Bergetto's death from the Cardinal, we might expect there to be some awkwardness between them when they are both invited to Soranzo's birthday celebrations at the end of the play. However, the shocking events that follow seem to reconcile the two men. Donado greets the Cardinal's command that Putana's body be burnt with ''Tis most just' (V.6.135). This punishment of a greater crime seems to appease him.

CHECK THE BOOK

Ford may have borrowed this structure from *Hamlet*. At the end of Act III, Polonius is accidentally killed. The death of this pompous but well-meaning comic character creates a sense of increasing doom.

CONTEXT

Florio is also the name of John Florio, the author of an Italian-English phrase-book called *First Fruits* (1578) that Ford consulted when writing his play.

Richardetto is most significant in the play as a man who abandons the role of revenger. Having faked his own death, he returns to Parma in disguise in order to spy on his adulterous wife and to punish her lover, Soranzo. Yet Richardetto proves to be no great schemer. He adopts the disguise of a doctor so that he may insinuate himself into Florio's household, thus to find out more about the courtship between Annabella and Soranzo. He is therefore well placed to discover Annabella's pregnancy, and critics have sometimes wondered if he does so, keeping it a secret so that the marriage to Soranzo will go ahead to the latter's humiliation. More obviously, the main advantage of Richardetto's disguise as a doctor is the fact that it allows him to hand out drugs, including poisons. Doctors were often viewed with suspicion at this time, much like the Apothecary in *Romeo and Juliet*. Yet Richardetto proves himself cowardly and inept at exacting revenge. By getting Grimaldi to murder Soranzo at the exact same location where his niece, Philotis, is meant to be marrying Bergetto he is largely responsible for Bergetto's death. It is intriguing that this fact never comes to light in the course of the play. When Richardetto casts off his disguise at the end and promises to tell of what he has seen, we might wonder whether he will leave this detail out. More generally, Richardetto's function in the play seems to be to bear witness to the fact that Heaven's justice is at work in the death of Hippolita, thus rendering his own revenge schemes unnecessary. He is also a moral commentator, summarising the action of the play as 'the effect of pride and lust at once/ Brought to shameful ends' (V.6.152–3).

Philotis is a minor character whose motivations are barely sketched in. Like her uncle, Richardetto, she seems to represent a turning away from moral corruption. Where he abandons revenge to avoid the fate of Soranzo, Philotis rejects marriage and sexual fulfilment in order to avoid the fate of Annabella. Richardetto has clearly encouraged Philotis to woo Bergetto (III.5.27–8). His motives are not stated but seem likely to be financial, particularly since, as her parents are dead, Philotis is left on his hands. But although Philotis' affections are directed to this end, there seems also to be some genuine affection and some sexual attraction between herself and Bergetto and she weeps to see him die in Act III Scene 7. Her decision to enter a nunnery could have reflected her grief at Bergetto's death, but Ford makes it clear that it is dictated by

CHECK THE BOOK

It is possible that Ford's audience would have remembered the fate of Ophelia in *Hamlet*. When Hamlet tells her (cruelly, even sarcastically) to 'Get thee to a nunnery' (III.1.123), she does not comply. In retrospect, it might have been better if she had, just as Philotis is apparently 'saved' by Richardetto's intervention.

Richardetto. He insists that it is too dangerous for her in the world and that 'Who dies a virgin lives a saint on earth' (IV.2.27–8). Philotis meekly concurs and disappears from the play.

THEMES

INCEST

Incest is one of the very last 'deviant' sexual practices still deplored by Western civilisation. It provokes feelings of disgust as well as a kind of prurient fascination and, in this respect, today's theatre audiences probably differ little from those who first watched *'Tis Pity She's a Whore*. The definition of incest, however, seems to have been considerably more complicated in the seventeenth century.

Perhaps the single most important difference was the fact that, as well as those related by blood, those related by marriage, for example, brothers and sisters-in-law, parents and their stepchildren, could be accused of incest. Indeed, this accounts for most of the accusations recorded in the sixteenth and early seventeenth centuries.

Nevertheless, the definition of what constituted an incestuous relationship had been historically unclear for some time. When Henry VIII married his sister-in-law, Catherine of Aragon, he cited the Bible – *Deuteronomy* 25:5–10 – which encourages a man whose brother has died to marry the widow and beget children to perpetuate his memory. But when Henry wanted a divorce, he was able to turn to another part of the Bible (*Leviticus* 18:6), in which marriage is forbidden between 'any that is near of kin', including a brother and his sister-in-law.

Obviously, there was a problem if the Bible could not be made to agree on exactly what degree of relationship constituted incest. Nor did history offer any clarification. In Ancient Athens, a man could marry his half-sister; in Ancient Egypt, full siblings were allowed to marry. In the early Christian church, St Augustine had advocated a hard-line approach, prohibiting the marriage of uncle and niece and of first cousins (unlike *Leviticus* which allowed both) but by the mid-sixteenth century in England, the law had been changed so that first cousins could now marry. Such historical disagreement suggested that

> **CONTEXT**
>
> It may be that Ford was inspired to write *'Tis Pity* by the case of Sir Giles Allington who was put on trial in 1631 for marrying the daughter of his half-sister. His penalty was notoriety and an extremely harsh fine of £12,000.

the prohibition against incest was based on shaky foundations that were subject to redefinition. There was no reliable and universal law. Hence, in *'Tis Pity She's a Whore* Giovanni has some historical basis for his argument that it is only 'a peevish sound,/ A customary form, from man to man,/ Of brother and of sister' that is the bar ''twixt my perpetual happiness and me' (I.1.24–7).

Moreover, in Ford's lifetime there seems to have been a considerable discrepancy between the terms of moral outrage that described incest and the leniency with which it was punished. Until 1650, along with other immoral practices including adultery, fornication and drunkenness, incest was prosecuted by the ecclesiastical courts rather than by the secular courts of law, which meant that it was punished only by public penance. This involved the offender standing in the parish church, dressed in penitential white, with a placard bearing the words 'for incest'. Then, in front of the congregation, they would confess their sin and ask for forgiveness. This may have been a terrible humiliation but it was far preferable to the physical punishments given out by the secular justice system, including whipping and branding for prostitutes, or death by hanging for thieves.

In fact, there were very few prosecutions for incest in the late sixteenth and early seventeenth centuries in England. This may be because it occurred only rarely, because it remained a secret, because it was a crime that did not unduly trouble local authorities or a combination of all three. It seems likely that incest was more common then than it is now, if only because families lived in much greater physical proximity to one another. For example, it was usual for close relatives of the opposite sex to share a bed. In his sermons on incest, delivered between 1616 and 1626, Arthur Lake, Bishop of Bath and Wells, pointed out that if God had not created a kind of sexual aversion between close relatives, incest would be hard to avoid for 'the necessary cohabitation of Parents and Children, Brethren and Sister, would yield too much opportunity and be too strong an incentive unto this unlawful conjunction'. Equally, the distance between brothers and sisters during childhood might have encouraged sibling incest. It is a well-documented fact that siblings brought up apart, perhaps not even knowing of the other's existence, are often sexually drawn to one another as adults. In the

---

CONTEXT

In *'Tis Pity She's a Whore*, Ford never explains why Annabella does not recognise her brother when she sees him from her balcony in Act I Scene 2. It is possible that they have not lived together for many years and that Giovanni's return from university marks their sudden, renewed intimacy.

early modern period, this separation may have been the norm. The practice of sending boys out of the home, first to a wet-nurse, then to school or an apprenticeship, and then to work or university meant that siblings could be relative strangers to one another, though closely tied by blood.

Incest had been a sensational theme on the public stage for two decades before Ford wrote *'Tis Pity*. Beaumont and Fletcher's play *A King and No King* (1611) deals with brother-sister incest. Yet the couple never acts on their desire and at the end (as is appropriate for a tragi-comedy) the 'siblings' turn out not to be related after all. John Webster's *The Duchess of Malfi* (1613) examines a sibling relationship that is clearly marked with incestuous yearning on the brother's part but, again, this desire is never consummated (though Ferdinand's subsequent madness and the murder of his sister clearly anticipate Giovanni's actions). In Thomas Middleton's *Women Beware Women* (1621), there seems to be repressed desire between the brother and sister, Livia and Hippolito, but the incest that is sexually consummated is between Hippolito and his niece.

Ford's *'Tis Pity She's a Whore* looks back to these earlier plays in its treatment of incest but it is much more daring. Annabella and Giovanni remain siblings until the end of the play – a closeness in blood that would have made them a clear-cut case of incest. The physical consummation of their desire also distinguishes them from these other brothers and sisters who merely yearn. Nevertheless, the play still reflects some of the uncertainty about incest that Ford's society experienced.

On the one hand, there is the uncompromising denunciation of this crime by the Friar and the Cardinal. On the other, there is Giovanni's powerfully romantic rhetoric of 'One soul, one flesh, one love, one heart, one all' (I.1.34), and the Friar's admission that if there were no God, and man were led solely 'by Nature's light' (II.5.31), incest might even be defensible. Moreover, there is a distinct lack of legal redress for incest in the play. Annabella is punished at the hands of her lover, but this is hardly a punishment for incest, since Giovanni's hatred is directed at the moral qualms that have led her to repent of their love. Similarly, Giovanni's murder is plotted as punishment for adultery rather than incest and

CHECK THE BOOK

Incest has long been a subject for **tragedy**. Beginning with Sophocles' *Oedipus Rex*, the theme recurs in Shakespeare's *Hamlet* and Middleton's *Women Beware Women*, and more recently in Eugene O'Neill's *Mourning Becomes Electra* (1931) and Arthur Miller's *A View from the Bridge* (1955).

he is killed by the *banditti* who are themselves criminals. Only Putana is in any sense legally punished for condoning incest, and this comes after Vasques has taken the law into his own hands by having her blinded.

Perhaps it is simply that the play focuses on divine justice working through the characters on stage: Giovanni's transformation into a psychotic killer is itself a punishment for incest. Moreover, we would not necessarily expect a revenge **tragedy** to focus on the legal punishment of crimes since the **genre** is predicated on the corruption or inadequacy of human law. However, it is also possible that the play hints at an uncertainty about what the legal punishment of incest should be, or that it creates a fantasy in which incest is automatically exposed and violently punished as a kind of propaganda, perhaps in acknowledgement of the fact that the law was largely powerless to detect or to punish incest. At the same time, Ford seems to have gone out of his way to complicate an audience's response to incest, rationalising it, even romanticising it, allowing the spectator to rethink their moral outrage when presented with it.

FATE AND DAMNATION

> There is a place –
> List, daughter! – in a black and hollow vault,
> Where day is never seen. There shines no sun,
> But flaming horror of consuming fires,
> A lightless sulphur, choked with smoky fogs
> Of an infected darkness . . . (III.6.8–13)

This vivid depiction of hell, uttered by the Friar on a dark stage and lit by candlelight, terrifies Annabella and may have had a similar effect upon Ford's audience. But it also raises some important questions about the ultimate fate of the **protagonists**.

In the early modern period, the ways in which people thought about Hell and damnation were divided according to whether they were Protestant (the official religion of England) or Catholic (a form of worship prohibited but still secretly practised). For the Catholic, hell was a terrifying reality but it was one that could be avoided if the sinner were prepared to make the effort. Confession, absolution,

CONTEXT

Purgatory is the place between Heaven and Hell where Catholics believed the souls of those who had died in a state of grace would linger until their crimes had been atoned for. One of the most famous descriptions of Purgatory was by the fourteenth-century Italian poet, Dante Alighieri, in his poem *La Divina Commedia* (*Divine Comedy*), which Ford may have known.

and penance were all rituals that promised forgiveness and
ultimately salvation to the sinner. Even after death, prayer was
believed to be efficacious in shortening the amount of time that the
sinner spent in Purgatory, atoning for his sins before being allowed
into Heaven. For the Protestant, however, things were very
different. Purgatory did not exist, meaning that the sufferings of the
dead in the afterlife could no longer be affected by the living. More
frighteningly, according to the doctrine of a Protestant Reformer
called Jean Calvin, every individual's fate was already predetermined
and nothing he did in life could affect whether he went to Heaven
or Hell. This doctrine was called 'double predestination', meaning
that some would be saved (the 'elect') and others damned (the
'reprobate'), but the individual could never know which she/he was
until the moment of death. They might suspect one way or the
other, but they could neither be certain nor could they logically
predict which it would be since God was beyond the
comprehension of a mere mortal. Moreover, although God provided
grace to enable the sinner to repent he was also said to harden the
hearts of the reprobate so that she/he could not repent.

CONTEXT

We do not know
whether Ford
himself was a
Catholic or a
Protestant. His
poem, *Christ's
Bloodie Sweat*
makes reference to
'the elect', a
strictly
Calvinist/Protestant
term, but his use
of ritual in the
plays has often
been seen to echo
Catholic practices.
Many of his
patrons had
Catholic
connections. See
**Background:
John Ford's life
and works**.

'Tis Pity She's a Whore seems to follow the Catholic idea of
damnation as something that it is within the individual's ability to
avoid. The Friar insists to the incestuous, blasphemous Giovanni:
'The throne of mercy is above your trespass/ Yet time is left you
both' (II.5.64–5), but by the end of the play, whilst Annabella has
proven penitent and seems destined for Heaven, Giovanni appears
on stage as a murderer, a 'black devil' (V.6.90), doomed to Hell. It is
Giovanni's fate that raises the play's most persistent questions
about what it means to be doomed.

At the beginning, Giovanni argued that it was fate that made him
love Annabella. If that was damnable then 'the fates have doomed
my death' (I.2.140). The play clearly borrows from *Romeo and
Juliet* with its notion of 'star-crossed lovers' whose misfortune it is
to love someone wholly inappropriate, meaning that their love will
also bring about their ruin. The fact that Annabella and Giovanni
are brother and sister and their love incestuous makes them far
more accursed than either Romeo or Juliet. Yet the idea of 'fate' is
also questioned in the course of the play. We might doubt whether
Giovanni ever really wanted to be purged of his desire for

Annabella, considering that he has consistently defended incest. After his attempt at penance fails in Act I Scene 2, Giovanni never again expresses regret or contrition but glories in his incestuous love. For the Friar, Giovanni's malevolent fate is his own invention. What really damns him is not the impressive number of crimes he commits – idolatry, blasphemy, incest, murder – but his refusal (and perhaps his inability) to repent. The Friar suggests that his own prayers for Giovanni have had no effect because the latter is in a state of 'despair'. Despair was a sin for both Catholics and Protestants. It meant that the sinner lacked the faith to believe in God's mercy and to ask for His grace and was thus doomed by his/her own pride and self-loathing.

But what is perhaps most disturbing about Giovanni's end in the play is the hint of Calvinist predestination that surrounds it. Giovanni sees himself as impelled to his own destruction: 'Lost, I am lost: my fates have doomed my death' (I.2.140). The fact that God does not answer his prayers for forgiveness and purgation, and the fact that although the Friar promises grace Giovanni never receives it, might suggest that Giovanni is a 'reprobate' whom God has hardened so that he cannot repent. Giovanni's reckless immorality is then a consequence of his belief that he is damned whatever he does.

Tragedy, as a genre, always makes us ask what power it is that sends the tragic protagonist to his death – whether something in his or her character dooms him; whether it is astrology or fate; whether it is God punishing sin. Nevertheless, Ford seems to have had a particular fascination with the concepts of fate, providence and predestination, embedding them in his tragedies without feeling the need to clarify which is predominant.

MARRIAGE

Perhaps more than incest, the plot of 'Tis Pity She's a Whore seems preoccupied with marriage. As well as the detailed negotiations for Annabella's union, we have Hippolita's plans to remarry (first Soranzo and then Vasques); and Bergetto's wooing of Annabella and then Philotis. In all these courtships, the play reflects closely the marriage practices of seventeenth-century England.

CONTEXT

We do not know whether Ford was married himself. It is one of the many basic facts about him that has been lost. See **Background: John Ford's life and works**.

Marriage was fundamental to the perceived order and well-being of society at this time. Sermons read in church every Sunday reminded the congregation that marriage was 'instituted of GOD, to the intent that man and woman should live lawfully in a perpetual friendship, to bring forth fruit, and to avoid fornication' (*Homily of the State of Matrimony* [1563]). But it was also an important means of social advancement. The fathers or guardians of the potential couple made the match with a view to uniting two families for their financial benefit (where the bride brought a large dowry) or for their ennoblement (where the bridegroom was a member of the gentry or aristocracy). The rise of a new middle class, wealthy and ambitious, in the late sixteenth century had coincided with the relative impoverishment of the aristocracy. Thus, it was advantageous to both to intermarry, as we see in *'Tis Pity She's a Whore*. Here, Florio is the self-made man eager to make an alliance with Lord Soranzo. His daughter may be scornfully referred to as 'Madame Merchant' (II.2.48), but presumably she brings enough wealth to pay off whatever debts this profligate nobleman has accumulated and she will provide him with an heir to continue his family line.

As well as reflecting on the motives for marriage, Ford's play dramatises the process by which courtships were undertaken and marriages contracted. Florio and Donado agree upon the financial benefits of the proposed union before Annabella and Bergetto have even met. It is Bergetto's inadequacy as a wooer, in the rituals of writing love-letters, giving presents, and meeting face-to-face, that prevents this courtship from progressing. The next stage of courtship, the betrothal or 'hand-fasting', takes place between Soranzo and Annabella. This was a much more binding contract than engagement is today and often mirrored the marriage ceremony by requiring the presence of a priest or some parental figure, the exchange of rings, and a spoken expression of consent – for example: 'I take thee for my husband'. Where Soranzo and Annabella are unusual is in the speed with which their wedding is subsequently performed. Normally, after the betrothal there was a period of at least two weeks in which the marriage banns had to be read in the parish church. Yet it was possible to pay for a special licence to make the interim briefer and this seems to be what Florio has done, rushing Annabella and Soranzo into marriage just two days after their betrothal.

> **CONTEXT**
>
> Once the contract had been sexually consummated, it was a legally-binding marriage, whether or not it was subsequently ratified by the Church. This is the kind of union that the Duchess and Antonio effect in Webster's *The Duchess of Malfi*.

> **CONTEXT**
>
> Shakespeare, too, had a very brief interval between his betrothal and his marriage – presumably because his bride, Anne Hathaway, was already six months pregnant.

Critical approaches

CONTEXT

Penthea may have been based on a real person, Lady Penelope Devereux (1562–1607). She had been forced to break her betrothal to Charles Blount, Lord Mountjoy, when young and had been married against her will to Robert Rich, Earl of Warwick. During the marriage, she had a number of illegitimate children by Mountjoy and when her husband divorced her, to the great scandal of the court, she married him. Ford seems to have admired Penelope, for he also dedicated his poem *Fame's Memorial* to her in 1606.

Ford's play, then, reflects his interest in the practical business of arranging marriages. Yet it also suggests his fascination with the misery and suffering that a bad marriage can bring. In *The Broken Heart* (1633), Ford had criticised the practice of enforced marriage. The play's two **protagonists**, Penthea and Orgilus, are already betrothed when Penthea's brother forces her to marry someone else, resulting in a union that she describes as adultery. Subsequently, Penthea starves herself to death and Orgilus takes his bloody revenge.

The situation is less straightforward in *'Tis Pity She's a Whore*: marriage may be forced upon Annabella by her pregnancy, but she admits that she might be able to love Soranzo and had earlier promised to choose him if she married anyone. Nevertheless, marriage is central to all of the play's revenge plots. Where it succeeds, it proves a source of shame and anger because the bride is not what she appeared to be, inspiring revenge. Where it fails, it brings about the participants' destruction. For example, Hippolita is so angry at Soranzo's refusal to marry her that she plots to kill him and ends up killing herself. Grimaldi's failure to win Annabella's hand in marriage causes him to make an attempt on Soranzo's life only to murder Bergetto, who was, incidentally, on his way to get married.

Marriage is invariably disastrous in Ford's **tragedies**. In this context, the improvised betrothal between Giovanni and Annabella, in which they exchange vows and kisses, appears both as a transgression against lawful marriage but also as a possible alternative. Uttered secretly, these vows inspired by love contrast strikingly with the public business of marriage, dictated by materialism, jealousy and lust.

ITALY

'Tis Pity She's a Whore is set in Parma, an Italian city in Lombardy, north of Rome. It was renowned in the seventeenth century as a flourishing centre of trade and is just the kind of place where a merchant like Florio could come to prominence. But why did Ford choose an Italian city rather than London?

Tragedies in early modern England were invariably located outside their country of origin – in Italy, France or Spain. This was partly to ensure that no comparisons could be made between the political situation within the play and that in the world outside the theatre. It also reflected the fascination and the fear that these Catholic nations (and Italy in particular) evoked in Protestant England.

From the late sixteenth century onwards, collections of Italian stories telling of erotic obsession, political intrigue and murder had flooded into England, inspiring some of the most famous plays of this period. Travel literature also contributed to the material available. It described the great beauty of Italy and the pleasures to be had from its art, architecture, music and dancing, but also issued a stern warning. As one writer cautioned in 1617, the traveller in Italy was in danger of learning 'the art of atheism, the art of epicurising [fine dining], the art of whoring, the art of poisoning, the art of sodomy'.

The stereotypical Italian was particularly defined by his potential for hypocrisy and political intrigue, as informed by a political tract called *Il Principe* (*The Prince*) published in 1532 by Niccòlo Machiavelli. It described how the successful ruler must maintain an appearance of virtue and religious devotion, whilst doing whatever was required to hold on to power, including committing murder. Most notorious was the Italian's skill at poisoning which allowed him to murder from a distance, without ever being caught, and was thus considered the most underhand of methods. The effect of poison, working secretly within the body, having infected the victim through some everyday object, also strengthened the idea of Italian hypocrisy.

The play draws on these assumptions about Italy in a number of ways. It emphasises the Catholicism of Parma through the presence of the Friar, the Cardinal, and references to the Pope in Rome, and by the practices of confession and absolution. Yet, it is much less concerned than many earlier plays with satirising or vilifying Catholicism (see **Characterisation: Friar**). Many of the play's characters have Italian names, but their personalities are also distinctively 'Italian', particularly Soranzo and Grimaldi who reflect the assumption that Italians were naturally passionate, quick to love or anger, and plagued by jealousy. Just as in *Romeo and Juliet* passions erupt into fighting against the backdrop of a long-running feud, so brawling seems to be a habitual part of Parmesan life. But above all, Italy is the appropriate setting for a play that

CONTEXT

Romeo and Juliet, *Othello*, *The Duchess of Malfi* and *The White Devil* were all derived from Italian stories, some of them based on actual historical events. One of the most influential collections was the *Decameron* (1353) by Giovanni Boccaccio which contained one hundred violent and bawdy tales.

includes four different revenge plots, two involving poison. So self-conscious is the play about this connection that, just before he is expelled from Parma, Vasques rejoices that 'a Spaniard out-went an Italian in revenge' (V.6.145–6).

DRAMATIC GENRE

'Tis Pity She's a Whore draws on two specific **genres**, popular on the Jacobean stage, namely revenge tragedy and city comedy. It is these genres that dictate the kinds of characters we find in the play, as well as the actions it represents.

REVENGE TRAGEDY

Revenge tragedy is a form of drama that became extremely popular in England in the late 1580s. It focuses on a terrible crime – usually the murder of a father or a son – for which no legal justice can be obtained because the authority figure with the power to punish is implicated in the crime. The revenger suffers a moral dilemma in deciding to take revenge: he knows that it is against the law and the teachings of Christianity but he feels that he has no choice. Nevertheless, revenge is always punished and although the revenger is successful in killing his enemies, he too must die at the end.

'Tis Pity She's a Whore follows the Jacobean form of revenge tragedy in which there are multiple plots and the crime to be avenged is sometimes relatively minor. Frustrated love rather than political ambition is the main motive that links these plots, although a sense of dishonour is also prominent in the revenge of Soranzo and Giovanni. The means by which revenge is achieved varies, again suggesting Ford's debt to earlier plays. For example, Grimaldi's poisoned sword and Hippolita's poisoned wine both recall the final scene of *Hamlet*. The fact that Hippolita gains access to the wedding feast by performing in a masque is also conventional. In Thomas Kyd's *The Spanish Tragedy* (1587), the villains are killed when they act in a tragedy written by the main revenger, Hieronimo. In Thomas Middleton's *The Revenger's Tragedy* (1607), Vindice kills his enemies in the middle of a masque.

Nevertheless, Ford's play is also marked by its abortive revenge plots, just as it is defined by abortive marriages (see **Themes: Marriage**). For example, Richardetto abandons his plot against Soranzo in Act IV Scene 2 when he sees that the heavens are working for him. Similarly, although Donado's failure to gain justice for his nephew's murder is exactly the scenario that might have led to revenge, he does not pursue it. This avoidance of revenge is not simply attributable to concerns about its immorality. *'Tis Pity* does not seem overly interested in this debate, perhaps because by 1631, all the arguments for and against were painfully familiar and the revenger did not usually bother to rehearse them. The dramatist's challenge was to make revenge new, either by combining more and more revenge actions into one play or by making the revenge itself more bloody and sensational. Ford seems to have preferred the latter approach, but the sheer number of revenge plots initiated, if not completed, in *'Tis Pity* also suggests his interest in revenge as a means of structuring the play (see **Critical approaches: Structure**).

> **? QUESTION**
> In Griffi's 1973 film of the play, Hippolita, Grimaldi and Richardetto are all cut. What effect do you think the loss of these characters and their revenge plots would have on Ford's tragedy?

CITY COMEDY

Considering Ford's obvious indebtedness to revenge tragedy for the themes and structure of *'Tis Pity*, it is perhaps surprising to find that comedy also exerted a powerful influence over the play.

From about 1605, the English stage was dominated by 'city comedy', a new kind of drama that focused on merchants and the gentry pursuing their own greed and social advancement in the city of London, often through the making of advantageous marriages. For example, in Thomas Middleton's comedy, *A Chaste Maid in Cheapside* (1613), the heroine, Moll, is to be married off to a wealthy lord, Sir Walter Whorehound (an adulterer much like Soranzo) but she outwits her father (an ambitious merchant) to marry the man she loves. Ford clearly knew Middleton's work, because he borrowed the comic subplot from his tragedy, *Women Beware Women*. This subplot involved a beautiful and intelligent young woman being courted by a childish idiot called the Ward, who was controlled by his greedy uncle. Here, we see the origins of Bergetto and Donado in *'Tis Pity She's a Whore*.

CONTEXT

The 'gull' or fool was a standard comic character, the victim of a deception that tricked him out of money or an inheritance. Most of Ben Jonson's comedies have multiple gull or fool characters, for example *Volpone* in which a merchant, a lawyer, an old man, and a noblewoman are tricked into believing that they will be made the heirs to Volpone's fortune.

CONTEXT

For further discussion of the **genre** of the play see Verna Foster's essay, ''Tis Pity She's Whore* as City Tragedy' in *John Ford: Critical Re-Visions*, ed. by Michael Neill (Cambridge UP, 1988), pp. 181–200.

More generally, the location, characters and structure of *'Tis Pity* are all familiar from city comedy. Ford emphasises the competitive, mercantile world of Parma, where gallants wear the latest fashions and visit puppet-shows and prostitutes, and where brawls occur in the street outside someone's house, causing complaints about the noise. The characters seem largely drawn from comedy, for example, the trickster servant (Vasques), the braggart soldier (Grimaldi), the greedy merchant (Florio) and the foolish gull (Bergetto). Moreover, the multiple plots (originating from the attempts of three suitors to win Annabella's hand) represent not just the themes (greed, marriage, trade) but also the multi-layered structure of comedy.

The play's tragic conclusion gains some of its power, then, from its overthrowing of comic conventions. Florio has tried to balance his desire to make a socially advantageous marriage for his daughter with his desire for her to be happy. He wants to keep Donado as his friend, but he expresses relief when Annabella turns Bergetto down. He is totally unprepared for the discovery of incest and murder in his midst, for Parma is not the kind of place where such things happen. Right until the moment of his death, Florio cannot comprehend that he is in a tragedy rather than a comedy. Equally, we might argue that the strange fact that Vasques escapes any punishment but exile, despite the fact that he has plotted and executed a series of murders, is a throwback to the play's comic heritage in which the witty servant usually avoided severe punishment.

STRUCTURE

'Tis Pity She's a Whore was written in five acts. If we look closely, we can see other structural patterns at work, suggesting that Ford designed it with great care.

The play divides naturally into two parts, with a break at the end of Act III.

The first part ends with the murder of Bergetto and the failed attempt to get justice. This anticipates what is to follow in two ways. Firstly, the murder of an innocent man (one of the play's few comic characters) seems to signal a shift from tragi-comedy to tragedy. Secondly, it suggests that justice is temporarily unavailable in a world of corrupt authority figures but that it may yet come through divine intervention. At the end of Act III, Florio promises that 'Heaven will judge them for't another day' (III.9.69) and the second part of the play partially fulfils this expectation. Heaven is praised for punishing Hippolita's murder attempt, Giovanni and Annabella's incest, and Soranzo's revenge.

An alternative place to divide the play, as suggested by the Mermaid edition's editor, Martin Wiggins, would be after Act IV Scene 1. Here, Annabella and Soranzo are married and Hippolita's plot to murder Soranzo fails. The scene ends with the Friar's ominous prophecy: 'that marriage's seldom good,/ Where the bride-banquet so begins in blood' (IV.1.107–8). The second part of the play then opens with news that the marriage is already showing signs of tension (IV.2.10–11) and brings it to its catastrophic conclusion. By placing the break here, we can also see more clearly the play's pattern of celebration interrupted by murder; love intruded upon by hate. Part One features the marriage banquet at which revenge fails but Hippolita is killed. Part Two features the birthday banquet, at which two revenge plots succeed and no less than three characters are killed. Ultimately, the way in which the play is divided (where, in performance, the director places the interval) will determine which aspect of the play she/he wishes to emphasise: its providential structure, showing the failure to achieve justice and then its success; or the pattern of society disrupted by revenge.

There are, however, other structural patterns at work in the play, particularly the way in which the two main actions – the incest plot and the revenge plot – are put together. The incest plot is characterised by scenes limited to just two characters. For example, Giovanni and the Friar argue about incest in Act I Scene 1 and Act II Scene 5. Then, as Giovanni increasingly evades the Friar's reach, he is replaced by Annabella, who has private meetings with the Friar in Act III Scene 6 and Act V Scene 1. What interrupts the privacy of this plot, and its pattern of two-character scenes, is Annabella's pregnancy and the necessity of marriage. The secret vows of Annabella and Giovanni are replaced by her betrothal to Soranzo, witnessed by others, followed by the public wedding and

CHECK THE BOOK

Most of Shakespeare's plays also divide up in this way. The end of Act III is where directors usually place the interval in performance.

CHECK THE BOOK

Ford is famous for his dramatic technique of interrupting celebration with tragedy. In *The Broken Heart* (c.1631), a dance to celebrate a marriage is interrupted three times by the news that someone has died (V.2).

feast. Thus, the incest plot remains essentially linear, but gradually widens out to include more participants.

By contrast, the revenge action of the play is characterised by a proliferation of small plots, which rise to prominence and then fall from sight, rather than remaining a consistent subtext to the action. For example, there is no revenge in Act I, but in Act II we find Hippolita, Richardetto and Grimaldi arranging Soranzo's murder. These plots are further developed in Act III but by Act IV Scene 2, they have dissolved: Hippolita is dead, Grimaldi has been sent to Rome and Richardetto has placed his trust in Heaven. Act IV, however, sees a new and more deadly strain of vengeance introduced into the play. Soranzo and Vasques's revenge plot is more ambitious since it has two intended victims – Giovanni and Annabella (three, if we count Annabella's unborn child). Moreover, it inspires a kind of pre-emptive retaliation from Giovanni. His plot to kill Soranzo is the final revenge action of the play, occurring late in Act V. It is here that revenge and incest meet.

QUESTION

In Griffi's film, the play's poetry is modernised and translated into prose but much of Ford's **imagery** is retained. Do you think *'Tis Pity* would be easy to adapt in this way? Does this tell us anything about Ford's style?

LANGUAGE

WORDS AND IMAGES

CHECK THE NET

Lisa Hopkins has published a useful essay on the theme of knowing in *'Tis Pity* in the Spring 1998 edition of the online journal *Renaissance Forum.* Go to **www.hull.ac.uk/ renforum** and click on the link to back numbers. The article can be found in Volume 3, Number 1.

Ford's language has often been praised for being plain and concise, but it is also famously obsessive. The same words or images are referred to again and again, in some cases attaining such reality that they become visual spectacles or even objects on stage. The most obvious example in *'Tis Pity* is the heart, which begins as a figure of speech and ends up as a bloody thing on the end of Giovanni's dagger. Before discussing the heart in more detail, however, it is worth considering two other repeated words that are thematically central to the play, namely 'know' and 'blood'.

The word 'know' and its related forms recurs seventy-six times. This frequency is hardly surprising considering how many secrets the characters are trying to hide, and the urgency with which they are finally revealed. At the end of the play, Giovanni insists on telling his story, 'that times to come may know/ How as my fate I honoured my revenge' (V.6.35–6). Yet the word 'know' also resonates in other contexts. In the first scene, Giovanni appears to know too much, or at least to have attained the wrong kind of knowledge. He questions some of the central beliefs of Renaissance society. Hence, the play has sometimes been linked to *Dr Faustus* and *The Atheist's Tragedy* by Cyril Tourneur as a 'tragedy of knowledge'. Another reason why the word 'know' recurs so frequently in the play is its association with sexual experience: to 'know' someone sexually. This can sometimes undermine the characters' intended meaning to suggest their darker motivations. For example, Giovanni tries to defend himself from the accusation of lust, but the fact that he uses the word 'know' implies his guilt: ''Tis not, I know,/ My lust, but 'tis my fate that leads me on' (I.2.154–5).

'Blood' is another word that resonates throughout the play in a variety of contexts. It is the shared genetic inheritance that Giovanni believes joins him to Annabella (I.1.31–2). It is the source, in the body, of passions including lust and anger, as Soranzo asserts: 'All my blood/ Is fired in swift revenge' (IV.3.149–50). Furthermore, 'blood' can also be a **metaphor** for social rank, as when Soranzo concedes that Grimaldi is 'My equal in thy blood' (I.2.37–8, see **Contemporary perspectives: A cultural materialist reading**). At the same time, blood is a physical substance that we see on stage – Annabella uses it to write her letter; it pours from Bergetto's wound; it covers Giovanni's clothes in the final scene. Thus, the word 'blood' anticipates bloodshed, but it also provides a motivation for it. Characters act out of 'blood', that is out of lust, anger and the need to defend the honour of their family.

Finally, the play's most persistent image is the heart. This is the origin and token of love: 'Soranzo is the man that hath her heart' (II.3.49). It is also a symbol of sincerity and truth, for it was supposed to have the possessor's feelings actually engraved upon it. Thus, when Soranzo wants to discover the identity of Annabella's lover he threatens: 'I'll rip up thy heart/ And find it there' (IV.3.53–4). As the play progresses so the **imagery** surrounding the heart becomes increasingly violent and morbid, making it inevitable that Giovanni should finally rip open Annabella's breast and display her heart. At the same time, the heart as represented on stage, a bloody piece of meat, is not at all how it was linguistically described. It cannot tell us to whom it belonged let alone what its presence means (See **Extended commentaries: Text 3**).

CHECK THE BOOK

In Ford's **tragedy** *Love's Sacrifice* (1632), Bianca tells Fernando: 'When I am dead, rip up my heart and read/ With constant eyes, what now my tongue defines,/ Fernando's name carv'd out in bloody lines' (II.4.93–5).

Ford's repetition of key words and images contributes to the play's sense of tragic inevitability. It also develops the themes that make that tragedy meaningful.

STYLE AND TONE

By comparison with other Cavalier dramatists, for example Thomas Carew and William Davenant, who were praised for their extravagant language, Ford's style has often appeared understated. Yet there are two notable exceptions in 'Tis Pity, specifically the lush lyricism of Giovanni and Annabella, and the violent invective directed against them.

Giovanni's descriptions of Annabella are strongly influenced by **Petrarchan** poetry. This style, which idealised the beloved as beautiful and unattainable, and described the lover's sufferings as a mixture of agony and ecstasy, derived from the fourteenth-century Italian poet, Francesco Petrarch. His **sonnet sequence**, the *Canzoniere* ('Song-Book'), had been written between 1327 and 1374 but was still being imitated in England three hundred years later. The object of Petrarch's praise was Laura whose beauties he described in the form of a **blazon**. In 'Tis Pity, we find Giovanni using the blazon in praise of Annabella:

> Such a pair of stars
> As are thine eyes would, like Promethean fire,
> If gently glanced, give life to senseless stones . . .
> The lily and the rose, most sweetly strange,
> Upon your dimpled cheeks do strive for change . . . (I.2.191–5)

The conceits of eyes like stars and of a red-and-white complexion that mingles the lily and the rose (symbolic of chastity and desire) clearly reflect Petrarch's praise of Laura. Similarly, although Annabella mocks Giovanni's elaborate compliments, she deploys Petrarchan **imagery** herself. When she stands on her balcony and sees Giovanni below, she cries: 'But see, Putana, see; what blessed shape/ Of some celestial creature now appears?' (I.2.127–8).

This likening of the beloved to a celestial figure also reflects other features of Giovanni's lyricism, namely its references to classical mythology and to **Neoplatonic** ideas, which were intended to

CONTEXT

'Cavalier' is a term used to describe the supporters of Charles I during the English civil war. It is usually applied to poets and dramatists in this period, often courtiers, who wrote with a particularly flamboyant style on decadent or immoral themes. See also **Literary background: Caroline drama**.

CHECK THE BOOK

In *Romeo and Juliet*, we also find the comparison of eyes like stars when Romeo sees Juliet on her balcony: 'Two of the fairest stars in all the heaven,/ Having some business, do entreat her eyes/ To twinkle in their spheres till they return' (II.1.57–9).

elevate the lovers to the status of the divine. For example, Annabella's forehead is apparently fairer than that of Juno (I.2.188–90); and when they kiss 'Thus hung Jove on Leda's neck/ And sucked divine ambrosia from her lips' (II.1.16–17). Giovanni uses a familiar Neoplatonic argument – that beauty is virtuous and inspires virtue – to justify their love in Act II Scene 5, lines 18–23.

In stark contrast is the language that Soranzo and Vasques use against the lovers. Soranzo delivers his insults in verse, as befits a man of his rank, but the language seethes with hatred and revulsion:

> Come, strumpet, famous whore! . . .
> Harlot, rare, notable, harlot . . .
> Was there no man in Parma to be bawd
> To your loose, cunning whoredom else but I?
> Must your hot itch and pleurisy of lust,
> The heyday of your luxury, be fed
> Up to a surfeit, and could none but I
> Be picked out to be cloak to your close tricks,
> Your belly-sports? Now I must be the dad
> To all that gallimaufry that's stuffed
> In thy corrupted bastard-bearing womb? (IV.3.1, 4, 6–14)

Soranzo imagines sexual desire as though it were indistinguishable from venereal disease – both are characterised by a 'hot itch' and lead to fever or 'pleurisy'. The unborn child is no more than a hideous, fleshy growth, 'that gallimaufry that's stuffed/ In thy corrupted, bastard-bearing womb' (IV.3.13). Perhaps most striking are the aural effects of this passage. Soranzo's insults keep jarring the flow of the **iambic pentameter** line. For example, 'harlot' and 'strumpet' are **trochaic** rather than iambic, thus creating a harsh, discordant rhythm and one that keeps forcing a break in the middle of the line (called a **caesura**). The speech is also full of hard consonants: the **plosive** 'b' sounds of 'bawd', 'belly' and 'bastard-bearing' and the more subtle and insidious 'l' sounds of 'lust', 'luxury', 'cloak' and 'close'.

There is, then, a stark contrast between the long, flowing, elegant lines of Giovanni in which he expresses his love, and the vicious, disjointed verse of Soranzo's hatred. Yet the harshest language of all

CHECK THE BOOK
Romeo also likens Juliet to a 'bright angel' and 'winged messenger of heaven' in their balcony scene (II.1.68, 70).

is that of Vasques. As is appropriate to a servant, Vasques speaks in prose, but his abrupt and colloquial speech also implies his lack of empathy and tendency towards violence:

> Come, sirs, take me this old damnable hag, gag her instantly, and put out her eyes ... Gag her, I say! S'foot, d'ee suffer her to prate? ... I'll help your old gums, you toad-bellied bitch!
> (IV.3.224–5, 228–30)

Vasques' use of contracted forms – 'd'ee' ('do ye'), 's'foot' ('By God's foot') – reflects his haste but it also creates an ugly aural effect, suggesting his contempt for those he addresses. Perhaps most striking is the bestial imagery by which he degrades Putana, in particular 'toad-belled bitch' which also hints at his secret loathing of a woman past her sexual prime, whose body has been altered by child-bearing.

To summarise, we might note that the two extremes of language in Ford's play – the lyrical poetry and the brutal prose – are both inspired by the characters' opposing attitudes towards incest. Those who seek to defend the act (and the love behind it) do so through poetic language; those who deplore and condemn it make use of a lower register. **Ironically**, the more the lovers are verbally abused the more the audience may be inclined to sympathise with them.

STAGING

If the language of *'Tis Pity She's a Whore* is defined by its visceral images, the play in performance is defined by a small number of macabre props. These include the cup from which Hippolita drinks poison, the blood that pours from Bergetto's wound, the letter written in blood that Annabella drops from her window, and, of course, the heart. As discussed above, these stage properties literally embody the preoccupation with 'blood' and 'heart' at the level of language. They also emphasise the play's obsessive focus on the body and its secrets.

In general, the play makes interesting use of the spaces provided in the theatre in which it was originally staged. The balcony is used at

---

CONTEXT

Although they differ from the theatres for which Ford wrote, Shakespeare's Globe Theatre in London and the Swan Theatre in Stratford are two fine examples of reproduction Elizabethan and Jacobean playhouses. If you manage to see a play at one of these, think about how the upper stage and the discovery space are used.

least three times: once when Annabella and Putana look down on the suitors (Act I Scene 2), once when Giovanni watches Annabella's courtship by Soranzo (Act III Scene 1), and once in Act V Scene 1 when Annabella drops the letter. In the first two instances, the fact that the characters are placed *'above'* suggests their detachment from and their superior knowledge of the other characters. Yet this impression is quickly undermined by the necessity that they come down on to the stage. Rather than standing aloof from love, Annabella descends to meet incestuous passion in what is a kind of moral and spiritual fall. Where Giovanni adopted a position of command up on the balcony, declaring himself 'regent' of the fates (III.2.20), he is forced to come down when Annabella falls ill, making him appreciate that he is not in control of their destiny. Annabella's final appearance on the balcony further reinforces this point. She is locked into her chamber, fearing that she is about to become a victim of revenge, and has to rely on a passer-by to deliver her warning to Giovanni. Her visual height at this point is **ironic**.

> **? QUESTION**
> How does Ford's staging echo Shakespeare's *Romeo and Juliet*? You might think, for example, about Annabella on the balcony and the representation of her bedchamber on stage.

'Tis Pity She's a Whore also uses the discovery space to important effect. The discovery space was the curtained area at the back of the stage, between the two doors, which could be used to reveal particular scenes or images. For example, in *The Spanish Tragedy*, Hieronimo pulls back the curtain to reveal his son's corpse. In *The Tempest*, the curtain reveals two people, presumed to be dead, playing chess. In *'Tis Pity She's a Whore*, the discovery space may have been used for Annabella's repentance in Act III Scene 6. The stage direction is unusually elaborate: *'the Friar in his study sitting in a chair, Annabella kneeling and whispering to him, a table before them and wax-lights; she weeps, and wrings her hands'*. Ford clearly wants his audience to look at this highly emblematic scene first, before we hear any words spoken. In fact, the players may often have reverted to the discovery space to stage intimate, domestic scenes: Soranzo's study in Act II Scene 2, for example, and, perhaps initially, Annabella's bed in Act V Scene 5. However, the curtain was also a notorious place for spies or murderers to lurk behind and it is probably from here that the *banditti* emerge to kill Giovanni in Act V.

Lighting effects are another particular feature of *'Tis Pity She's a Whore*. In the big open-air theatres, performances always occurred during daylight so darkness had to be described rather than simulated on stage. In the small, indoor theatres for which Ford wrote, however, it was possible to create darkness and Ford takes advantage of this in scenes such as Annabella's confession and, more importantly, Bergetto's murder. It may be that here the stage was plunged into almost complete darkness for characters and audience alike, so that it is only when, as the stage direction tells us, Poggio and Officers enter *'with lights'* that the extent of Bergetto's injury is revealed. He suggests before this that it is so dark that he cannot tell whether the liquid spilling from him is urine or blood (III.7.11–12).

CHECK THE FILM

For an example of how this staging worked, see John Madden's film, *Shakespeare in Love* (1998). Before Gwyneth Paltrow's character, Viola, becomes involved, the production of *Romeo and Juliet* includes a boy playing Juliet and an adult male playing the Nurse.

Finally, it is important to remember that there were no actresses in English theatre companies at this time. Annabella was first played by a woman in 1661. Until then, the parts of Annabella, Hippolita and Philotis would have been played by boys, with Putana played by either a boy or an adult male actor.

PART FOUR

CRITICAL HISTORY

ORIGINAL RECEPTION

There are no first-hand accounts of *'Tis Pity She's a Whore* as it was originally performed in 1631. The earliest comment comes from the famous diarist, Samuel Pepys, who described a production he saw in 1661 as 'a simple [i.e. foolish] play, and ill acted'. Nevertheless, some of the quartos of 1633 allude to the play's popularity, with the title-page describing 'the general commendation deserved by the actors in their presentment of this tragedy'. That the tragedy itself was admired is attested to by Thomas Ellice, one of Ford's literary circle, in a dedicatory poem printed in some editions of the quarto and reproduced on page 42 of the New Mermaids edition.

The pleasure that Ellice took in the play seems to have centred on Annabella. His poem opens with the lines 'With admiration I beheld this Whore/ Adorned with beauty'. He could not have confused the beauty of an actress playing Annabella with the character since, until 1661, the role was played by a boy. It was the *idea* of Annabella that exerted a powerful attraction. Nevertheless, Ellice seems to have responded with the same conflicted feelings of moral disapproval and sympathy that characterise audience responses to Annabella today (see **Reading *'Tis Pity She's a Whore***). He ends his poem assuring Ford that his fame will live on through *'Tis Pity She's a Whore*, 'and Annabella be/ Gloriously fair, even in her infamy' (lines 9–10).

CRITICAL HISTORY

'Tis Pity She's a Whore has always been considered one of Ford's major works, alongside *The Broken Heart* and *Perkin Warbeck*, but as Ford's body of work is comparatively small this is not very surprising. He composed only eleven plays without a collaborator, three of which are now lost, as opposed to the more than thirty each of Shakespeare and Shirley, and he has languished in reputation and popularity behind the great Elizabethan dramatists.

CONTEXT

Thomas Ellice was probably the brother of Robert Ellice, a member of the Inns of Court, to whom Ford dedicated his play *The Lover's Melancholy*. We might therefore expect him to be complimentary.

CONTEXT

James Shirley (1596–1666) was one of the most prolific playwrights of the Caroline period, writing more than thirty plays between 1625 and 1642. He was also chief dramatist for the Queen Henrietta's Men, the company who performed *'Tis Pity She's a Whore*.

Since the 1960s, however, there has been a marked revival of interest in Ford's work and in this play in particular. The negative terms by which Ford had been traditionally denigrated – decadent, sensationalist and derivative – have been challenged by critics and redefined. Furthermore, the moral **ambiguity** of Ford's work, its suspicion of authority and its rejection of gender stereotypes have all seemed to make *'Tis Pity She's a Whore* more relevant to the twenty-first century. This discussion of the critical history of the play will begin with its negative reputation, before considering how the play relates to two key theoretical approaches: feminism and cultural materialism.

'Decadence' is a term that haunts any critical discussion of Ford's work and of *'Tis Pity She's a Whore* in particular. It means decay, decline, a kind of falling-off from a state of excellence and vitality. More colloquially, the term suggests self-indulgence or irresponsible pleasure that borders on immorality. Ford was certainly interested in decay as a theme. As a writer of **tragedy** he could hardly have been otherwise since tragedy, by definition, considers the fall of a great individual. At the beginning of the play, the Friar laments the decline he has seen in Giovanni. Similarly, in *The Broken Heart*, a young woman sinks into despair and starves herself to death; her former lover succumbs to revenge and is bled to death. The 1994 Royal Shakespeare Company's production of *The Broken Heart*, directed by Michael Boyd, made this theme of decay strikingly apparent. The stage design included a table set with a lavish banquet, including a swan as decoration. Subsequently, when the banquet was shown again, the feast was decaying, the swan had been strung up and disembowelled, and the noise of flies could be heard.

 CHECK THE BOOK
For photographs from this production and a review, see Kristin Crouch, '"The Silent Griefs Which Cut the Heart Strings": John Ford's *The Broken Heart* in Performance' in Edward J. Esche (ed.), *Shakespeare and his Contemporaries in Performance* (Ashgate, 2000).

Nevertheless, the decadence of Ford's work is more commonly seen as a moral defect rather than an artistic choice. The fact that Ford makes incest central to his play, and that he treats it sympathetically, suggested to many nineteenth-century critics that his own morality must be at fault. Kenneth Tucker summarises the perspective of two of *'Tis Pity She's a Whore*'s early editors, William Gifford (1827) and Hartley Coleridge (1840), suggesting that although they admired Ford's 'powerful scenes and beauteous lyrical passages', they also found them 'to be unforgivably besmirched by prurient interests and a generally unwholesome moral outlook'. If this moral decay did not lie in Ford himself, then it must have lain in his audiences. In the 1930s, Una Ellis-Fermor and H. J. Oliver suggested that Ford was a writer of psychological insight and some subtlety, but that he was restricted (even corrupted) by theatrical fashion and audience expectation. As Oliver explains,

> The methods by which the Elizabethan playwright sought to affect his audience were certainly not weak in the first place; as a result, a still stronger stimulus was needed by 1630 if that audience was to be stimulated at all . . . That is why the Caroline dramatist turned more and more for his subject matter to the daring, the immoral, the unnatural; that is partly why Ford, among others, sought subjects like incest and adultery and was content to have Giovanni appear with Annabella's bleeding heart on his dagger. (*The Problem of John Ford*, p. 3)

CHECK THE BOOK
See H. J. Oliver, *The Problem of John Ford* (Melbourne UP, 1955).

Finally, Ford seems to have been condemned as decadent simply because he was writing after a period of extraordinary inventiveness and imagination in the history of English drama. Ford's tragedy, with its self-absorbed, incestuous lovers, performed for an aristocratic audience in the 'private' theatres, has been argued to reflect the decadence of the Cavalier world as it headed inevitably towards destruction in the English Civil War (see **Literary background: Caroline drama**).

One of the major reasons for an upswing in Ford's critical fortunes has been critics' willingness to challenge these assumptions, beginning with the dramatist's supposed immorality. Again, this argument has a long history. Havelock Ellis in 1888 defended Ford as a rebel against the establishment, arguing that he used incest to challenge conventional ideas of morality, rather than merely for gratification. In 1968, Mark Stavig also defended Ford by insisting that '*Tis Pity* does have a strong moralistic framework, and that Ford's audience would never have assumed he was condoning incest:

CHECK THE BOOK

See Mark Stavig, *John Ford and the Traditional Moral Order* (University of Wisconsin Press, 1968).

In making [Giovanni] an incestuous lover, a blasphemous atheist, and a sensational murderer, Ford makes his problems so extreme that an audience would inevitably feel less emotionally involved. (*John Ford and the Traditional Moral Order*, p. xvii)

The idea that it was Ford's audience that was morally decadent, and that the dramatist had to betray his own finer feelings in pandering to it, has also met with some sharp rebukes. This is where the term 'sensationalism' is often invoked, describing an art that has set out to shock its audience, and to produce intense feelings such as horror or fear, often by means of scenes of violence or bloodshed. The term is usually derogatory, suggesting that the sensation is purely intended as entertainment – it does not have any moral or intellectual value. But although Oliver may be right that Ford was under pressure from his audience to increase the bloodshed, this is not to deny that Ford's violent spectacles are meaningful in themselves. In the 1930s, the French writer and theatre producer Antonin Artaud celebrated *'Tis Pity She's a Whore* as an example of the 'Theatre of Cruelty'. This was a type of drama that rejected psychological realism and over-reliance on the written word in favour of a more physical theatre, characterised by visual spectacle and sound. The play's violence, in particular, would cut through complacency and self-deception (*The Theatre and its Double* [Calder and Boyars, 1970], pp. 18, 21).

 CHECK THE NET

For a famous example of the saint depicted as a swooning lover, and of an angel as a kind of Cupid, see Gian Lorenzo Bernini's sculpture of *The Ecstasy of St Teresa* (1652) reproduced at **www.artchive. com/artchive**. Find the link to Bernini and then click on 'View Image List' to locate the sculpture.

More recently, critics have demonstrated how emblematic was the violence depicted upon the English Renaissance stage, meaning that it came replete with philosophical, religious and/or moral significance. For example, the notorious heart-on-a-dagger would have recalled the martyr's heart pierced by God's love, as well as a more erotic version featuring Cupid. The pierced heart could also be a symbol of envy, a meaning that sits nicely with Giovanni's feelings regarding Soranzo at the end of the play. In his essay 'Sensationalism and Melodrama in Ford's Plays', Richard Madelaine argues that Ford's sensational effects are neither gratuitous nor superficially related to the play. He describes the image of the heart on a dagger as 'dramatis[ing] the essential nature of the passion that is the play's subject. The violence and gore of the image are part of its thematic point, as is the shocking literalism of its use of a real heart as a symbol of the real nature and literal consequences of this kind of passion' (*John Ford: Critical Re-Visions*, p. 33).

Finally, the notion of Ford as a derivative writer, 'decadent' in the sense of coming after a period of literary greatness, has also undergone a significant change. Rather than merely list the details that Ford borrowed as evidence of his indebtedness, critics have revealed how creative and ironic is Ford's appropriation of Shakespeare. In his essay '*Love's Sacrifice*: Ford's Metatheatrical Tragedy' (*John Ford: Critical Re-Visions*), Martin Butler argues that Ford's allusions to Shakespeare were intended for the pleasure of a highly-literate audience from the Inns of Court. The changes that he made to Shakespeare resulted in a play that 'flaunt[s] its intertextuality and constantly draws attention to the deliberate flaws in its mimetic surface' (p. 6). One of the most recent editors of the play, Simon Barker, describes it as a kind of deconstruction of *Romeo and Juliet*:

> What was *repressed* in *Romeo and Juliet* and in traditional criticism, where the emphasis is on order and unity, control and moral orthodoxy, *surfaces* in Ford's reordering of Shakespeare's dramatic world. ('*Tis Pity* [1997], p. 114)

According to Barker, Ford's play is much darker than Shakespeare's, depicting sexuality itself as something deviant and destructive, and replacing the providential narrative of *Romeo and Juliet* with an increasingly sceptical vision (see **Literary background: Ford and Shakespeare**).

CONTEMPORARY PERSPECTIVES

Finally, we might look beyond the morality of the play, its sensational stage effects and its derivativeness, to consider '*Tis Pity She's a Whore* as actively engaged with its own historical moment. Two of the most influential perspectives on English Renaissance drama are feminism and cultural materialism and it is through these readings of '*Tis Pity She's a Whore* that the play's concerns with gender and with class come into focus.

CHECK THE BOOK

The range of meanings for this symbol has been discussed in an important essay by Michael Neill, '"What Strange Riddle's This?": Deciphering *Tis Pity She's a Whore*' in *John Ford: Critical Re-Visions* (Cambridge UP, 1988), pp. 153–79.

CHECK THE BOOK
For useful introductions to these theoretical perspectives, see Peter Barry's book *Beginning Theory* (Manchester, 1995).

CHECK THE BOOK
Julie Sanders' and Alison Findlay's works are good examples of feminist readings of Renaissance texts. See Sanders, *Caroline Drama: The Plays of Massinger, Ford, Shirley and Brome* (Ashgate, 1999) and Findlay, *A Feminist Perspective on Renaissance Drama* (Blackwell Publishers, 1999).

A FEMINIST READING

Feminist criticism examines the representation of women in literature. It considers how power relations between men and women are constituted, with women being constructed as different (and invariably inferior) to men and how this perception of difference satisfies the needs and desires of individual men and of society. Finally, it considers how language 'makes what is social and constructed seem transparent and "natural"' (Barry, *Beginning Theory*, p. 134).

This approach has proven particularly fruitful in relation to the work of John Ford. As Julie Sanders summarises in her study *Caroline Drama: The Plays of Massinger, Ford, Shirley and Brome*:

> What has partly defined [Ford's] drama for the twentieth century are his incredibly self-willed, if ultimately defeated heroines: Eroclea in *The Lover's Melancholy* (the only one of his female protagonists who survives to the end of the play, and a conscious reworking of the Shakespearean heroine), Penthea and Calantha in *The Broken Heart*, Annabella in *'Tis Pity* and Katherine Gordon in *Perkin Warbeck*, to name but a few. (p. 7)

It is not only the emotional and psychological complexity of these female characters that has attracted attention but the historical insights they afford into the conditions of women in Ford's own time. For Sanders, Ford shows 'a very real recognition of the plight of women in his contemporary Caroline society, controlled as they were by the head males of the family in private and by patriarchy at large in the public sphere' (p. 26).

Annabella is one of the most intriguing characters in this respect because, like Giovanni, she rebels against moral and social conventions, freely expressing and acting on her own desires. Yet her position differs radically from his. She is increasingly confined, often visibly so – first, in the narrow forbidding space of the Friar's cell, then in her own chamber where she has been imprisoned by Soranzo, and finally in the arms of her lover, Giovanni, who kisses and then kills her. Above all, Annabella seems to be restricted by the stereotypes of virgin and whore by which she is persistently defined. Alison Findlay argues in her book *A Feminist Perspective on Renaissance Drama*:

> Annabella is constructed as a figure of desire and of sacrifice by the men around her. Unlike [Giovanni], she does not have the power to fashion herself. All she can do is to negotiate a pathway between the various roles laid out for her by the male characters. (p. 25)

Findlay demonstrates how Annabella tries to seize the initiative and manipulate the roles available to her. For example, in Act IV Scene 3, she plays the part of the Virgin Mary, transforming her pregnancy into an immaculate conception, Giovanni into God, and Soranzo into an aggrieved Joseph: 'Let it suffice that you shall have the glory/ To father what so brave a father got' (IV.3.44–5). This appropriation of the biblical female ideal empowers Annabella, whilst at the same time parodying the Catholic Church and endorsing Protestant suspicions of the cult of virginity. Ultimately, however, Annabella's triumph is only temporary. Her being reduced to the heart on the end of Giovanni's dagger (her body left offstage) is the ultimate symbol of her lack of self-determination and of her objectification by men. The fact that Giovanni brings Annabella's heart to the men-only banquet dramatises the extent to which 'Annabella is the feast on which they have all fed to satisfy their desires . . . It is they who have constructed her, consumed her, sacrificed her independence by offering her only a narrow choice of parts to play' (Findlay, *A Feminist Perspective*, p. 31).

Although little has been written on Hippolita and Putana, we might extend this reading to them also. Hippolita is a particularly valuable subject for feminist analysis because the assumptions that other male characters make about her are so clearly at variance with what she says about herself. Particularly revealing is Vasques' mistrust that he uses to justify her murder. He recalls how he 'promised her fair, but I knew what my reward should have been, and would willingly have spared her life but that I was acquainted with the danger of her disposition' (IV.1.78–81). But Hippolita never suggests that she was planning to betray Vasques, nor does she seem inherently or indiscriminately dangerous. Hippolita is

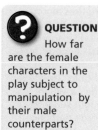

QUESTION
How far are the female characters in the play subject to manipulation by their male counterparts?

demonised by Vasques, perhaps as an expression of his own class resentment and misogyny, but also as a reflection of his culture's suspicion of the adulteress, and of any woman whose desire escaped the bounds determined by social morality.

CHECK THE BOOK

See Roberts, 'The Crone in English Renaissance Drama', *Medieval and Renaissance Drama in England* 15 (2002), 116–37.

CONTEXT

England's change from Catholicism to Protestantism meant that to become a nun was no longer seen as a desirable vocation for a young, unmarried woman. In Shakespeare's *A Midsummer Night's Dream*, Theseus describes it to Hermia: 'For aye to be in shady cloister mewed,/ To live a barren sister all your life,/ Chanting faint hymns to the cold fruitless moon' (I.1.71–3). The relative approval that Philotis' fate seems to meet with in *'Tis Pity She's a Whore* might suggest Ford's Catholic sympathies.

In fact, it might be argued that all the female characters (with the exception of Philotis) represent a dangerous transgression of the accepted roles for women. Annabella is, for the first half of the play, sexually unchaste but not married; Hippolita is both a widow and a wife; Putana is a female 'tut'ress' (I.2.67) who advocates incest. It may also be significant that Putana is old. In an essay entitled 'The Crone in English Renaissance Drama', Jeanne Addison Roberts describes how elderly women were either 'trivialised, sexualised or demonised' when represented on the stage. She explains:

> In such societies, where women are valued for their sexual relationship to men and their powers of propagation, men are likely to ignore the crone as unnecessary, to regret her as a social burden, to be repelled by their imagination of her voracious and unproductive lust, to fear her as a reminder of death . . . (p. 120)

Putana's punishment at the end of the play seems so disproportionate to her crime that we might view it as a final expression of the anxieties represented by the rebellious female who does not fit into the social categories of maid, wife or widow, virgin or whore. More generally, the play demonstrates and exposes an overwhelming urge by the figures of male authority, including Giovanni himself, not only to control and to punish female desire, but also to categorise and to label women – hence the play's title. This seems potentially to extend to all the women of the play except Philotis, who only escapes by becoming a nun.

A CULTURAL MATERIALIST READING

Cultural materialist critics examine a literary text for what it reveals about the political struggles of the past, whilst using it to challenge assumptions about hierarchy and power relations in the present. In other words, these critics look for the political messages behind a text, and relate these to modern day conflicts. The reference to 'materialism' emphasises the notion that all literary works are produced by their particular historical and political moment: they are the literary material of the time in which they are written. Until recently, most criticism of Ford's work tended to assume that it was largely apolitical, that Ford was 'primarily a purveyor of theatrical pleasures and offer[ed] no direct access to the real social relations of this time' (McLuskie, '"Language and Matter with a Fit of Mirth": Dramatic Construction in the Plays of John Ford' in *John Ford: Critical Re-Visions* (Cambridge UP, 1988), p. 124). *'Tis Pity She's a Whore* has been an important text for critics seeking to argue that Ford was, after all, fascinated by and implicated in, the class struggle that typified the 1620s and 1630s in England.

The section on **Caroline drama** examines the ways in which theatre of this period has been considered as slavishly following the opinions of the court and/or providing escapist entertainment for a largely aristocratic audience. Nevertheless, some arguments against this perspective have also been put forward. The work of Martin Butler in *Theatre and Crisis, 1632–42* has been extremely influential in this respect:

CHECK THE BOOK

See Butler, *Theatre and Crisis, 1632–1642* (Cambridge UP, 1984) and Clerico, 'The Politics of Blood: John Ford's 'Tis Pity She's a Whore', *English Literary Renaissance* 22 (1992), 405–34.

> The Caroline drama has been dismissed for its escapist tendencies; yet as a body it is perhaps most remarkable for its consistent, yet insistent political interests. It has been derided for its servility to an unpopular and intolerant regime; yet it is full of suspicion and hostility towards the court and courtiers . . . The playwrights were dramatising the conflicts and tensions at work in their society, embodying men's dilemmas and voicing their grievances, anxieties and frustrations. (pp. 280–1)

Although Butler does not discuss Ford's work, his redefinition of what Caroline drama is has been extended by other critics to include Ford. For example, Terri Clerico develops an illuminating discussion of class antagonism and intermarriage in an essay entitled 'The Politics of Blood: John Ford's *'Tis Pity She's a Whore'*.

Clerico argues that *'Tis Pity* reflects the fact that Ford's society was changing from one based on inherited status to one dominated by wealth. Social mobility was increasingly common, which is to say that a person could be born into one class and rise (or fall) into another. The most obvious means to effect this change was through

A CULTURAL MATERIALIST READING continued

marriage. The union of a merchant family with a gentry or noble family through marriage could be to their mutual advantage – the merchant obtained a title, land and a sense of inherited privilege; the aristocrat obtained cash which might allow him to keep his estate, and a wife to provide him with an heir. Yet such marriages were also frowned upon as a corruption of the noble bloodline.

Clerico considers the proposed marriage between Annabella, the merchant's daughter, and Soranzo, the aristocrat, arguing that the play reflects society's fear of class transgression and of social mobility. Hence, although incest is morally condemned, it is also imagined as socially desirable. Giovanni's physical union with his own sister is 'a defensive act . . . Incest comes to emblematise the desire to congeal class allegiances, to conserve the purity of class membership' (p. 416).

Yet, as Clerico points out, Giovanni is not a nobleman but rather the son of a merchant. Why should he be so concerned to preserve his bloodline? It is here that Ford's play can be seen not simply to reflect its social context but actively to engage with it. Clerico argues that Giovanni's incestuous desire, expressed through the imagery of blood, parodies 'the defensive strategies of the upper class . . . to confine its circulation to a rigidly proscribed social unit' (p. 424).

 CHECK THE NET
For further critical discussion of Ford's work, see the essays online at **www.luminarium. org/sevenlit/ford**

Clerico combines a historical reading of the play with close reading of the text's language to argue that Ford is actively commenting on his own society through '*Tis Pity She's a Whore*. This attempt to read Ford more politically suggests a new direction in the play's critical history, taking us even further away from the epithet 'decadent' with which Ford's work has so long been put down.

PART FIVE

BACKGROUND

JOHN FORD'S LIFE AND WORKS

Little is known about the life of John Ford, for he lived at a time when the details of only the most famous lives were recorded. From the documentary evidence that survives, we learn that he was born in April 1586 in Ilsington, Devon, the second son of Thomas Ford, a wealthy landowner. The family had connections with the legal profession – Thomas Ford's cousin was a judge – and this may partly explain why both John and his elder brother, Henry, went to study at the Middle Temple, one of the four famous law schools in London known collectively as the Inns of Court. Ford seems to have continued his association with the school, and may have practised law, until his death. One of his last published works in 1638 describes him as 'Master John Ford of the Middle Temple'. However, the Inns of Court were equally as famous for the literary and dramatic education they offered. Some of the most important dramatists of the Elizabethan and Jacobean periods, including John Marston and John Webster, studied here.

It was probably at the Middle Temple that Ford began his career as a writer. His first published work in 1606 was a poem entitled *Fame's Memorial* in honour of the Earl of Devonshire. Over the next ten years, he wrote a number of poems and prose tracts but it was not until the 1620s that he turned to play-writing, collaborating with other more established dramatists. This was not unusual. By far the majority of plays written for the Elizabethan and Jacobean stages were collaborations, sometimes by as many as five different dramatists each writing an act. It was a system favoured for its speedy delivery of new plays to feed the voracious appetite of the theatre-going public. Ford seems to have begun as writing-partner to the experienced dramatist Thomas Dekker, with whom he wrote a tragedy called *The Witch of Edmonton* (together with William Rowley) in 1621. There were at least another four plays from 1624 though only one has survived. It was also at this time that Ford forged a relationship with Shakespeare's acting company, the King's Men, whose principal dramatist was now

CONTEXT

It is possible that Ford attended Oxford University before the Middle Temple. There is a reference to a John Ford, a gentleman from Devon, entering Exeter College, Oxford, in 1601. It may be significant that both Exeter College and the Middle Temple were associated with Catholicism.

CONTEXT

John Webster (c.1578–1630) was a famous Jacobean playwright, best known today for two **tragedies** *The White Devil* and *The Duchess of Malfi*. His work was particularly influential upon Ford who wrote a dedication to the **quarto** edition of *The Duchess of Malfi*, praising it as a 'masterpiece'.

CONTEXT

John Fletcher's
(1579–1625)
popularity as a
playwright came
close to rivalling
Shakespeare's. He
rarely wrote alone
however; his most
famous
collaboration was
with Francis
Beaumont
(1584–1616) and
together they
produced several
extremely
successful
comedies,
tragedies and
tragi-comedies,
including *The
Maid's Tragedy*
(c. 1610) and *King
and No King* (1611).

John Fletcher. Ford wrote a tragi-comedy called *The Laws of
Candy* for them in the early 1620s, possibly based on another
dramatist's draft. After Fletcher's death in 1625, he worked
alongside John Webster and Philip Massinger to complete Fletcher's
last play, *The Fair Maid of the Inn*.

It was in the late 1620s, having served his apprenticeship and
ambitious to establish himself as a leading dramatist, that Ford
wrote those plays that would make him famous. The first three –
The Lover's Melancholy (1628), *The Broken Heart* (1629) and a play
now lost called *Beauty in a Trance* (1630) – were performed by the
King's Men at their small, indoor playhouse, the Blackfriars.
Subsequently, Ford seems to have changed his allegiance to another
'private' theatre, the Phoenix on Drury Lane, managed by
Christopher Beeston. There was competition and some antagonism
between these two theatres in 1630, and Ford may have felt that his
writing style was better suited to the Phoenix than to the more
elaborate 'Cavalier' drama performed at the Blackfriars. *'Tis Pity*
(1631), *Love's Sacrifice* (1632), *Perkin Warbeck* (1633), and *The
Fancies, Chaste and Noble* (1635) were all performed by the Queen
Henrietta's Men, at the Phoenix. Ford's last play, *The Lady's Trial*
(1638) was performed there by a company of boy actors known as
Beeston's Boys. From 1629 onwards Ford's major tragedies were
published as **quartos**, in the case of *'Tis Pity She's a Whore* overseen
by Ford himself, thus ensuring his lasting fame as a dramatist.

Nevertheless, there are many aspects of Ford's life and opinions
that we might wish to know more about. Was he married? Did he
have children? When and in what circumstances did he die?
Recently, it has been speculated that Ford had Catholic leanings, at
a time when Catholic worship was prohibited by law, and that he
was politically sympathetic to the plight of the aristocracy under an
increasingly autocratic monarch, Charles I (see **Historical
background**). Unfortunately, the only remaining access we have to
Ford's personality is through his dedications (though these tell us
little other than his desire to seek patronage), and a few lines in a
poem from 1632, published by William Heminges. The latter was a
member of the King's Men who at least knew Ford and described
him: 'Deep in a dump Jack Ford alone was got/ With folded arms
and melancholy hat'. To be 'in a dump' means to be sullen and the

action of standing with one's arms crossed was symbolic of the melancholy lover. Whether or not Ford himself displayed these qualities, his reputation rests on his skill as a tragedian, one particularly concerned with the sufferings of frustrated love.

HISTORICAL BACKGROUND

Ford's life traverses the reigns of three monarchs: Elizabeth I (1558–1603), James I (1603–25) and Charles I (1625–49). As we will see, the period that had perhaps the greatest and most obvious influence on Ford's literary career was the Elizabethan, however it is important to know more about the years in which he established himself as a dramatist, 1625–39, known as the Caroline period after the monarch Charles I. These years are inevitably seen as the calm before the storm. This is because, in 1642, England was plunged into a series of civil wars between the supporters of Charles I (called Royalists or Cavaliers) and Parliament (the Roundheads or Puritans). These ended with the execution of the king in 1649 and the establishment of England as a republic under the leadership of the Protector, Oliver Cromwell. If, as seems likely, Ford was dead by 1639, he could not have experienced this trauma for himself. Yet the causes of the discord between King and Parliament were certainly manifest during his lifetime.

Charles inherited from his father, James I, many of the problems that defined his reign. The Jacobean court had been frequently criticised for its conspicuous consumption, manifest through feasts and elaborate entertainments, at a time of high unemployment and price inflation. It was also seen as morally decadent – James was notorious for his male favourites – and sex scandals undermined the ability of his court to set a good example. But, perhaps most importantly, it was James' assertion of royal privilege over the rights of the aristocracy and Parliament, and in defiance of English law, that created an increasingly anti-monarchical feeling in Stuart England.

On his succession, Charles was careful to bring about moral reforms at court. He and his queen, Henrietta Maria, emphasised the virtuous power of love and were often celebrated as the epitome of married chastity. Yet there were other aspects of James'

> **CONTEXT**
>
> In her short story, "'Tis Pity She's a Whore', Angela Carter deliberately confuses John Ford, the director of American Westerns such as *Stagecoach*, with John Ford the Caroline dramatist, by translating '*Tis Pity She's a Whore* into the Frontier land of nineteenth-century America.

kingship that Charles appeared to endorse and to repeat. Like his father, he had extravagant tastes, spending huge sums on staging masques at court, as well as amassing an impressive collection of art and sculpture. He also incurred considerable expenses through foreign policy, his military campaigns against Spain at the beginning of his reign proving to be costly failures. When the House of Commons refused to finance him (partly because of their mistrust of Charles' favourite, the Duke of Buckingham), Charles took his own unlawful measures to obtain the money. By levying taxes and forcing loans upon the wealthy he alienated both the common people and the nobility. When Parliament protested, Charles dissolved it in 1629 and ruled for eleven years without it, an obvious expression of his father's belief in the absolute power of the king. Finally, his stance on religion proved dangerously divisive. Although an Anglican himself, he was lenient about imposing anti-Catholic penalties, and his wife, Henrietta Maria, herself a French Catholic, encouraged expressions of this religion at court. More seriously, Charles appointed William Laud as Archbishop of Canterbury. Laud began to restore some 'Catholic' forms of ritual to the Church of England and to enlarge the power of the bishops, in direct opposition to the ambitions of the more radical Protestants, known as 'Puritans'. Charles' struggle to impose his own ideas about religion upon the Scottish Church led to war between the two countries, known as the Bishops' Wars of 1639–40, and subsequently to the English Civil War of 1642–9.

Ford was writing, then, at a time of political and social unrest, when the struggle for power between the king, the aristocracy and the House of Commons was becoming more acute, and when religious divisions were becoming increasingly political. The noblemen to whom Ford dedicated his works, including the dedicatee of *'Tis Pity She's a Whore*, John Mordaunt, Earl of Peterborough, were invariably either Catholic themselves or came from Catholic families. They were also outspoken against tyranny and the erosion of the rights of the aristocracy. By choosing them as dedicatees, Ford seems to imply some connection between his work and the interests of these parties.

LITERARY BACKGROUND

CAROLINE DRAMA

Caroline drama has long been considered a disappointment after the extraordinarily inventive and challenging theatre of the Elizabethan and Jacobean periods. Just as England in the 1630s is seen to be teetering on the brink of political crisis, so the drama of that period is overshadowed by its own disastrous climax. In 1642, all the theatres were closed by order of Parliament. But even without this knowledge of the theatre's doom, we can see that the theatrical landscape had changed considerably during Ford's lifetime.

Where in the late sixteenth century, the public theatres of the Globe, the Rose and the Swan had attracted an extremely varied audience, in the decade between 1620 and 1630 theatre seems to have become more of an exclusive and aristocratic taste. The new Caroline dramatists – Philip Massinger, James Shirley, John Ford and Richard Brome – wrote for the smaller, private theatres such as the Blackfriars, Salisbury Court and the Phoenix. These theatres charged higher admission prices, attracting a more 'genteel' audience. Another important change was the increasing influence of the court upon the organisation of the companies and their repertory. During Elizabeth's time, acting companies had been sponsored by leading aristocrats such as the Lord Chamberlain and the Lord Admiral, but by 1625 all the theatre companies were sponsored by a member of the royal family: Ford wrote for both the King's Men, now patronised by Charles I, and the Queen Henrietta's Men. The royal couple had a keen interest in theatre, particularly the queen who visited the Blackfriars and even acted herself, appearing at court in masques written to celebrate her virtues. Naturally, the royal couple wished to encourage plays that reflected their own values, for example, honour, chastity, and Neoplatonic love. The latter proved particularly influential, inspiring William Davenant's play *The Platonic Lovers* (1636) but also Ford's *Love's Sacrifice* (1629).

It is the deference of Caroline drama to royal authority that has since become problematic, encouraging critics to disregard the plays and masques as little more than propaganda. It has been

> **CONTEXT**
>
> In a masque called *Tempe Restored* by William Davenant (1632), the Queen performed the role of Divine Beauty.

> **CONTEXT**
>
> **Neoplatonic** love was a concept that had become extremely influential throughout Renaissance Europe. It argued for the spiritual dimension of both friendship and erotic love, suggesting that admiration of physical beauty in another person ought to lead to admiring the beauty of the soul, leading at last to love of God.

CAROLINE DRAMA continued

CONTEXT

The so-called 'Cavalier poets' included Robert Herrick, Sir John Suckling and Richard Lovelace, writing in the 1630s and 1640s. They were famous for poems which avoided politics to focus on the pleasures of drinking and sex, with an emphasis on the *Carpe Diem* ('Seize the day') theme, embodied by Herrick's poem, 'To the Virgins, to make much of time'.

argued that Caroline drama is too narrowly aristocratic, peddling a kind of escapist fantasy which allowed audiences to avoid confronting political and social tensions outside the theatre. The most popular **genres** were pastoral romance and tragi-comedy, dramatic forms that resolve tensions and avoid catastrophes often by supernatural means to create a highly seductive but highly artificial state of harmony. For this reason, Caroline drama has often been termed 'Cavalier' drama, thus likening it to the doomed supporters of Charles I. They similarly retreated into nostalgic visions of their own privilege rather than confronting the issues that would lead to war.

In the last few decades, however, this perspective has undergone considerable revision (see **Critical history**). It is now generally accepted that Caroline drama represents a wider range of perspectives than the so-called 'Cavalier', particularly in the plays written for the private and public playhouses which seem to have been more socially engaged and more critical of the monarch than had been previously thought. For example, Philip Massinger's tragedy *The Roman Actor* (1626) criticises the tyrannical Emperor Domitian for his use of censorship and explores the potential of theatre to inculcate virtue in its audience. Ford's history play, *Perkin Warbeck* (1633), has been seen as offering covert advice to Charles I, providing a model of kingship for him to follow. In the years when Parliament could not meet, the professional theatre may have provided a space for debate about issues surrounding royal power and its abuse, and the role of theatre in contemporary politics.

Nevertheless, it is hard to defend Caroline theatre from the charge that it was less vibrant and less productive than its Elizabethan and Jacobean predecessors. In 1624, there were thirty-six new plays, masques and academic dramas, but by 1630 this number had fallen to only nine. Instead, the fashion was to revive old plays, and even new plays were strongly imitative of their predecessors. For example, the city comedies of Middleton and Jonson strongly influenced Massinger's *A New Way to Pay Old Debts* (1621) and *The City-Madam* (1632). For his tragedy *The Traitor* (1631), Shirley borrowed the main plot from Middleton's *The Revenger's Tragedy* (1607). With *'Tis Pity*, Ford was busy appropriating scenes and plots from Middleton's *Women Beware Women* (1621) and Webster's *The Duchess of Malfi* (1613). But perhaps the most important influence on Caroline drama was Shakespeare and it is against this 'literary background' that we need to consider Ford's *'Tis Pity She's a Whore* in more detail.

FORD AND SHAKESPEARE

Ford referred to Shakespeare's plays for inspiration throughout his career. He invokes *Othello* in *The Queen, Love's Sacrifice* and *The Lady's Trial; King Lear* in *The Lover's Melancholy;* and *Richard II* in *Perkin Warbeck.* In the case of *'Tis Pity She's a Whore*, we find occasional echoes of *Hamlet* but also a consistent and skilful appropriation of two Shakespearean love **tragedies**: *Romeo and Juliet* and *Othello.*

> **CONTEXT**
>
> *'Tis Pity* is one of the only non-Shakespearean Renaissance plays produced by both the Royal Shakespeare Company (1977, 1991–2) and the National Theatre (1988).

Like *Romeo and Juliet, 'Tis Pity She's a Whore* focuses on a passionate love that must be kept secret from the lovers' families and from society at large. The lovers each have a confidant(e) – a Friar for the man, and a nurse/governess for the woman – who performs a similar function. The Friar is responsible for marrying the **protagonists** in *Romeo and Juliet*, and Annabella and Soranzo in *'Tis Pity She's a Whore*, but he is helpless to prevent the disaster that ensues. Both Juliet's Nurse and Putana encourage the love affair but from a comically amoral perspective. The Nurse recommends bigamy as a means of solving Juliet's problems; Putana encourages incest. Similarly, the role of the fathers is equivalent. Florio and Capulet both lament the fact that they have only one marriageable child (Florio assumes that Giovanni will not live long enough to be married (I.3.6–8)) and they are both determined that their daughters should marry for love. Their opinion changes later when their daughters fall sick though not for the reasons they assume (Juliet is grief-stricken at Romeo's banishment; Annabella is pregnant). Finally, we might note that both plays are located in an Italian city-state, that brawling and sword-fighting are common, and that poison is a means of death (see also **Themes: Italy**).

The influence of *Othello* is mainly confined to Soranzo's revenge and to Annabella's murder. For example, Vasques acts the part of Iago when he rouses Soranzo to violent fury and revenge against his wife, particularly when he perceives in him a tendency to pity (V.2.1–4). The distribution of roles within the revenge scheme also recalls *Othello*. Like Iago, the servant Vasques will kill the male

FORD AND SHAKESPEARE continued

lover and it is left to the husband, Othello/Soranzo, to deal with his adulterous wife. Finally, Soranzo's plan to have Annabella put on her wedding-dress before he kills her recalls Desdemona's choice of her wedding-sheets on the night of her death. At this point, Giovanni takes over from Soranzo in the role of Othello. Like Shakespeare's protagonist, he murders Annabella in her own bed, having first required her to pray so that her soul might go to heaven. Before stabbing her, he kisses her a number of times and then virtually quotes *Othello*:

Othello: I kiss'd thee ere I kill'd thee. No way but this –
Killing my self, to die upon a kiss. (V.2.361–2)

Annabella: What means this?
Giovanni: To save thy fame, and kill thee in a kiss. (V.5.83–4)

CHECK THE BOOK
Two detailed analyses of the function of Ford's borrowings in *'Tis Pity* are Robert Smallwood, *"Tis Pity She's a Whore* and *Romeo and Juliet'*, *Cahiers Elisabetháins* 20 (1981), 49–70 and Raymond Powell, 'The Adaptation of a Shakespearean Genre: *Othello* and Ford's *'Tis Pity She's a Whore'*, *Renaissance Quarterly* 48 (1995), 582–92.

Clearly, then, *'Tis Pity She's a Whore* is heavily indebted to Shakespeare's love **tragedies**. Yet this does not mean that Ford is guilty of either a slavish devotion to his predecessor or a lack of imagination. These self-conscious echoes have an important dramatic effect. For example, *'Tis Pity She's a Whore* asks its audience to remember *Romeo and Juliet* partly in order to create sympathy for the lovers. Rather than being divided by a feud, Ford's lovers are divided by biology which means that their love is even more 'star-crossed'. Equally, however, it is the differences between *Romeo and Juliet* and Ford's play that create a pleasurable sense of shock and even moral outrage in Ford's audience. This is not a love that is simply prohibited by an ancient feud; it is incest, a sin deplored by God and by society. Therefore, although Annabella and Giovanni may see themselves as Romeo and Juliet, their audience may not.

This creation of **ironic** difference is particularly strong in Ford's borrowings from *Othello*. By invoking the latter play, Ford is able to imply what Soranzo's revenge plans are in relation to Annabella – the decision to make her wear her wedding-dress becomes far more ominous. But when the murder is actually performed by Giovanni, the echoes of *Othello* become ironic. Annabella (unlike Desdemona) may have been adulterous but Giovanni is not the wronged husband in this play. Rather, it is he who has made a cuckold of Soranzo. Moreover, the *Othello* parallel also emphasises how violent is Giovanni's murder of Annabella. Othello was careful not to shed any of Desdemona's blood, wishing to preserve her beauty. When he discovered her innocence, he was so appalled he killed himself. By contrast, Giovanni makes a bloody spectacle of Annabella's heart and carves up her body with sadistic glee. Nor does he ever repent of his actions or commit suicide, though he is apparently glad to be killed.

In general, then, Ford cites Shakespeare to create assumptions about his characters and about the action of *'Tis Pity She's a Whore* that he can then fulfil or deny according to his own artistic intentions. There is no question that *'Tis Pity She's a Whore* succeeds as a play whether or not one has read *Romeo and Juliet* or *Othello*, but the deliberate echoes from the older plays add depth and irony to Ford's tragedy.

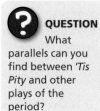

QUESTION
What parallels can you find between *'Tis Pity* and other plays of the period?

Historical Background	Ford's Life and works	Literary Background
1586 Trial of Mary, Queen of Scots	**1586** Birth of John Ford	
1587 Execution of Mary, Queen of Scots		**1587** Thomas Kyd's *The Spanish Tragedy*
1588 Defeat of the Spanish Armada		**1588** Marlowe's *Dr Faustus*
1595 Sir Walter Raleigh's voyage to Guiana		**1595** Shakespeare's *Romeo and Juliet*
1599 Essex fails to defeat rebels in Ireland		**1599** Opening of the Globe Theatre
	1602 Ford admitted to the Middle Temple to study law	
1603 Death of Elizabeth I; succession of James I		**1603** Shakespeare's *Othello*
1605 Gunpowder Plot is foiled		**1605** Ben Jonson's *Volpone*
	1606 Ford publishes *Fame's Memorial* and *Honour Triumphant*	
		1608 The King's Men take over the Blackfriars Theatre
		1612 John Webster's *The White Devil*
1613 Death of Henry, Prince of Wales, the heir to the throne of England	**1613** Ford publishes a religious poem, *Christ's Bloody Sweat* and a prose tract, *The Golden Mean*	**1613** Globe Theatre burns down; Webster's *The Duchess of Malfi*
1616 William Harvey discovers the circulation of the blood		**1616** Death of Shakespeare; Christopher Beeston builds the Phoenix Theatre
	1621 Ford collaborates with Dekker and Rowley on *The Witch of Edmonton*	**1621** Robert Burton publishes *The Anatomy of Melancholy*

Historical Background	Ford's Life and works	Literary Background
		1623 Publication of the First Folio, the first collected works of Shakespeare
1625 Death of James I and succession of Charles I	1625 Ford collaborates with Webster and Massinger on Fletcher's *The Fair Maid of the Inn*	1625 Death of John Fletcher
1626 Forced Loan controversy		1626 Queen Henrietta Maria acts in a Racine pastoral at court; Philip Massinger's *The Roman Actor*; Ben Jonson's *The Staple of News*
1628 Petition of Right submitted by Parliament; assassination of the Duke of Buckingham	1628 Ford writes *The Lover's Melancholy*	1628 Richard Brome's *The Northern Lass*
1629 Parliament dissolved; Personal Rule of Charles I begins (1629–40)	1629 *The Broken Heart* performed; *The Lover's Melancholy* is the first of Ford's plays to be published	1629 Salisbury Court theatre built; Ben Jonson's *The New Inn*
	1630 Ford writes *Beauty in a Trance* (now lost)	
	1631 *'Tis Pity She's a Whore*	1631 Death of John Donne; James Shirley's *The Traitor*
	1632 *Love's Sacrifice*	1632 Philip Massinger's *The City Madam*; Ben Jonson's *The Magnetic Lady*; James Shirley's *The Ball*; Richard Brome's *The Weeding of Covent Garden*

Historical Background	Ford's Life and works	Literary Background
1633 William Laud appointed Archbishop of Canterbury	**1633** Publication of *The Broken Heart*, *'Tis Pity She's a Whore* and *Love's Sacrifice; Perkin Warbeck* performed	**1633** John Donne's *Poems* published; William Prynne publishes an attack on the theatre called *Histriomastix* and is arrested and tortured
	1635 *The Fancies, Chaste and Noble*	**1635** Richard Brome's *The Sparagus Garden*
	1638 *The Lady's Trial* written and performed by Beeston's Boys	**1638** Publication of *Lycidas* by John Milton; Richard Brome's *The Antipodes*
1639 War between England and Scotland, the First Bishops' War (the Second occurs in 1640)	**1639** Publication of Ford's last play, *The Lady's Trial;* his death follows shortly afterwards?	
1642 Outbreak of the English Civil War		**1642** Theatres closed by Parliament
		1644 Second Globe Theatre pulled down in 1644
1649 Trial and Execution of Charles I; establishment of the English Commonwealth, headed by Oliver Cromwell		

Peter Barry, *Beginning Theory: An Introduction to Literary and Critical Theory*, Manchester UP, 1995

Fredson Bower, *Elizabethan Revenge Tragedy 1587–1642*, P. Smith, 1959

James Bulman, 'Caroline Drama' in *The Cambridge Companion to English Renaissance Drama*, ed. by A. R. Braunmuller and Michael Hattaway, Cambridge UP, 2003, pp. 344–71

Martin Butler, *Theatre and Crisis, 1632–1642*, Cambridge UP, 1984

Alexander Leggatt, *English Drama: Shakespeare to the Restoration, 1590–1660*, Longman, 1988

Ira Clark, *Professional Playwrights: Massinger, Ford, Shirley and Brome*, University Press of Kentucky, 1992

David Frost, *The School of Shakespeare: The Influence of Shakespeare on English Drama 1600–1642*, Cambridge UP, 1968

Richard A. McCabe, *Incest, Drama and Nature's Law, 1550–1700*, Cambridge UP, 1993

Kenneth Tucker, *A Bibliography of Writings by and about John Ford and Cyril Tourneur*, G. K. Hall, 1977

Julie Sanders, *Caroline Drama: The Plays of Massinger, Ford, Shirley and Brome*, Ashgate, 1999

Lawrence Stone, *The Crisis of the Aristocracy, 1558–1641*, Clarendon Press, 1965

LITERARY CRITICISM

Donald K. Anderson (ed.), *Concord in Discord: The Plays of John Ford, 1586–1986*, AMS Press, 1986

Donald K. Anderson, 'The Heart and the Banquet: Imagery in Ford's *'Tis Pity* and *The Broken Heart*', *Studies in English Literature* 2 (1962), 209–17

Antonin Artaud, *The Theatre and its Double*, Calder and Boyars, 1970

FURTHER READING

Terri Clerico, 'The Politics of Blood: John Ford's *'Tis Pity She's a Whore*', *English Literary Renaissance* 22 (1992), 405–34

Crouch, Kristin, '"The Silent Griefs Which Cut the Heart Strings": John Ford's *The Broken Heart* in Performance' in Edward J. Esche (ed.), *Shakespeare and his Contemporaries in Performance*, Ashgate, 2000

Dorothy Farr, *John Ford and the Caroline Theatre*, Macmillan, 1979

Alison Findlay, *A Feminist Perspective on Renaissance Drama*, Blackwell Publishers, 1999

Lisa Hopkins, *John Ford's Political Theatre*, Manchester UP, 1994

Ronald Huebert, *John Ford, Baroque English Dramatist*, McGill-Queens University Press, 1977

Gerald Langbaine, *An Account of the English Dramatick Poets*, Oxford, 1691

Clifford Leech, *John Ford and the Drama of His Time*, Chatto & Windus, 1957

Richard Madelaine, 'Sensationalism and Melodrama in Ford's Plays', *John Ford: Critical Re-Visions* (see below), pp. 29–54

Michael Neill (ed.), *John Ford: Critical Re-Visions*, Cambridge UP, 1988

H. J. Oliver, *The Problem of John Ford*, Melbourne UP, 1955

Jeanne Addison Roberts, 'The Crone in English Renaissance Drama', *Medieval and Renaissance Drama in England* 15 (2002), 116–137

Robert Smallwood, *''Tis Pity She's a Whore* and *Romeo and Juliet*', *Cahiers Elisabetháins* 20 (1981), 49–70

Mark Stavig, *John Ford and the Traditional Moral Order*, University of Wisconsin Press, 1968

Rowland Wymer, *Webster and Ford*, Macmillan, 1995

ADAPTATION AND FILMS

Angela Carter, ''Tis Pity She's a Whore', *Granta* 25 (1988), 179–98

Giuseppe Patroni Griffi (dir.), *'Tis Pity She's a Whore*, Italy 1973 allusion a passing reference in a work of literature to something outside the text; may include other works of literature, myth, historical facts or biographical detail

ambiguity the capacity of words and sentences to have double, multiple or uncertain meanings

aside when a character speaks in such a way that some or all of the other characters on stage cannot hear what is being said; or they address the audience directly. It is a device used to reveal a character's private thoughts, emotions and intentions

blazon a poetic description of a subject's virtues or physical beauties, listed one by one

caesura pause in the middle of a line of verse

dramatic irony when the implications of an episode or a speech are better understood by the audience than the characters

genre a type of literary work characterised by a particular form, style, or purpose

homonym one of a group of words pronounced or spelt in the same way but having different meanings

hubris excessive pride or self-confidence that seems to require punishment by the gods, often a cause of tragedy

iambic pentameter a verse line of ten syllables, in which five syllables are stressed, the emphasis falling on the second syllable in each word (iambic) e.g. 'machine', 'devour'. This is the verse form in which Shakespeare mainly wrote

imagery descriptive language which uses images to make actions or objects come to life

intertextuality the explicit or implicit referencing of other texts within a work of literature. It is designed to put the work in the context of other literary works and traditions and implies parallels between them

irony the humorous or sarcastic use of words to imply the opposite of what they normally mean; incongruity between what might be expected and what actually happens; the ill-timed arrival of an event that had been hoped for metaphor a figure of speech in which comparison is made between unrelated subjects. One subject might be described 'like' another, or it may be described 'as' another

mimetic imitative of real life, often used to describe the intention of art and literature

motif a recurring idea in a work, which is used to draw the reader's attention to a particular theme or topic

Neoplatonic A philosophical and religious system based on Plato which argues that everything in the earthly world is a reflection of an eternal world of higher truths or ideas. Earthly love and beauty can lead towards union with the divine

oxymoron a figure of speech in which words with contradictory meanings are brought together for effect

paradox a seemingly absurd or self-contradictory statement that is or may be true

parody to imitate another work of art or artist in order to ridicule them, often by exaggerating their style or features

pastoral a form of art that expresses a nostalgic view of the peace and simplicity of the life of shepherds in an idealised rural location

personification the treatment or description of an object or an idea as human, with human attributes and feelings

petrarchan a style of poetry based on the works of the fourteenth-century Italian poet, Francesco Petrarch, who published a series of love poems called the *Canzoniere* (1327–74) celebrating his love for a woman called Laura. Petrarchan poetry describes the lover's joy but also his frustration at desiring a woman who can never be his

plosive A consonant that is produced by stopping the airflow using the lips, teeth, or palate, and then suddenly releasing an outward flow of air (OED) e.g. *t, k, p, d, g, b*

protagonist the principal character in a work of literature

pun the use of words or phrases to exploit ambiguities and innuendoes in their meaning, a play on words quarto a relatively cheap book, consisting of pages where a single sheet of paper has been folded twice to produce four leaves

simile a figure of speech which compares two things using the words 'like' or 'as'

soliloquy a dramatic device which allows characters to speak directly to the audience as if thinking aloud, revealing their inner thoughts, feelings and intentions

sonnet a poem of fourteen lines, originating in Italy, usually on the theme of love. Sonnets were popular in England in the sixteenth century when they were composed by Sir Thomas Wyatt, Sir Philip Sidney, Edmund Spenser and Shakespeare among others

sonnet sequence a series of sonnets, usually written on the theme of love and linked together by narrative, by the recurrence of common themes, and/or by the identity of the speaker and the addressee

split-line a single line of verse which is divided more than once between different characters

symbolism investing material objects with abstract powers and meanings greater than their own; allowing a complex idea to be represented by a single object

tragedy in its original sense, a drama dealing with elevated actions and emotions and characters of high social standing in which a terrible outcome becomes inevitable as a result of an unstoppable sequence of events and a fatal flaw in the personality of the protagonist. More recently, tragedy has come to include courses of events happening to ordinary individuals that are inevitable because of social and cultural conditions or natural disasters

trochaic a metrical foot in which the first syllable is stressed and the second is unstressed, for example 'fifty', 'women'

wordplay verbal wit based on the meanings and ambiguities of words

Jane Kingsley-Smith studied for a degree in English Literature at Oriel College, Oxford, and for her PhD at the Shakespeare Institute, Stratford-upon-Avon. She has taught at the universities of Warwick, Salford and Hull and is now a lecturer at Roehampton University, London. She has published various books and articles on Shakespeare and his contemporaries.

NOTES

GCSE

Maya Angelou
I Know Why the Caged Bird Sings

Jane Austen
Pride and Prejudice

Alan Ayckbourn
Absent Friends

Elizabeth Barrett Browning
Selected Poems

Robert Bolt
A Man for All Seasons

Harold Brighouse
Hobson's Choice

Charlotte Brontë
Jane Eyre

Emily Brontë
Wuthering Heights

Brian Clark
Whose Life is it Anyway?

Robert Cormier
Heroes

Shelagh Delaney
A Taste of Honey

Charles Dickens
David Copperfield
Great Expectations
Hard Times
Oliver Twist
Selected Stories

Roddy Doyle
Paddy Clarke Ha Ha Ha

George Eliot
Silas Marner
The Mill on the Floss

Anne Frank
The Diary of a Young Girl

William Golding
Lord of the Flies

Oliver Goldsmith
She Stoops to Conquer

Willis Hall
The Long and the Short and the Tall

Thomas Hardy
Far from the Madding Crowd
The Mayor of Casterbridge
Tess of the d'Urbervilles
The Withered Arm and other Wessex Tales

L. P. Hartley
The Go-Between

Seamus Heaney
Selected Poems

Susan Hill
I'm the King of the Castle

Barry Hines
A Kestrel for a Knave

Louise Lawrence
Children of the Dust

Harper Lee
To Kill a Mockingbird

Laurie Lee
Cider with Rosie

Arthur Miller
The Crucible
A View from the Bridge

Robert O'Brien
Z for Zachariah

Frank O'Connor
My Oedipus Complex and Other Stories

George Orwell
Animal Farm

J.B. Priestley
An Inspector Calls
When We Are Married

Willy Russell
Educating Rita
Our Day Out

J. D. Salinger
The Catcher in the Rye

William Shakespeare
Henry IV Part I
Henry V
Julius Caesar
Macbeth
The Merchant of Venice
A Midsummer Night's Dream
Much Ado About Nothing
Romeo and Juliet
The Tempest
Twelfth Night

George Bernard Shaw
Pygmalion

Mary Shelley
Frankenstein

R.C. Sherriff
Journey's End

Rukshana Smith
Salt on the snow

John Steinbeck
Of Mice and Men

Robert Louis Stevenson
Dr Jekyll and Mr Hyde

Jonathan Swift
Gulliver's Travels

Robert Swindells
Daz 4 Zoe

Mildred D. Taylor
Roll of Thunder, Hear My Cry

Mark Twain
Huckleberry Finn

James Watson
Talking in Whispers

Edith Wharton
Ethan Frome

William Wordsworth
Selected Poems

A Choice of Poets

Mystery Stories of the Nineteenth Century including The Signalman

Nineteenth Century Short Stories

Poetry of the First World War

Six Women Poets

For the AQA Anthology:

Duffy and Armitage & Pre-1914 Poetry

Heaney and Clarke & Pre-1914 Poetry

Poems from Different Cultures

Key Stage 3

William Shakespeare
Henry V
Macbeth
Much Ado About Nothing
Richard III
The Tempest

Margaret Atwood
Cat's Eye
The Handmaid's Tale

Jane Austen
Emma
Mansfield Park
Persuasion
Pride and Prejudice
Sense and Sensibility

William Blake
Songs of Innocence and of Experience

Charlotte Brontë
Jane Eyre
Villette

Emily Brontë
Wuthering Heights

Angela Carter
Nights at the Circus
Wise Children

Geoffrey Chaucer
The Franklin's Prologue and Tale
The Merchant's Prologue and Tale
The Miller's Prologue and Tale
The Prologue to the Canterbury Tales
The Wife of Bath's Prologue and Tale

Samuel Coleridge
Selected Poems

Joseph Conrad
Heart of Darkness

Daniel Defoe
Moll Flanders

Charles Dickens
Bleak House
Great Expectations
Hard Times

Emily Dickinson
Selected Poems

John Donne
Selected Poems

Carol Ann Duffy
Selected Poems
The World's Wife

George Eliot
Middlemarch
The Mill on the Floss

T. S. Eliot
Selected Poems
The Waste Land

F. Scott Fitzgerald
The Great Gatsby

John Ford
'Tis Pity She's a Whore

E. M. Forster
A Passage to India

Michael Frayn
Spies

Charles Frazier
Cold Mountain

Brian Friel
Making History
Translations

William Golding
The Spire

Thomas Hardy
Jude the Obscure
The Mayor of Casterbridge
The Return of the Native
Selected Poems
Tess of the d'Urbervilles

Seamus Heaney
Selected Poems from 'Opened Ground'

Nathaniel Hawthorne
The Scarlet Letter

Homer
The Iliad
The Odyssey

Aldous Huxley
Brave New World

Kazuo Ishiguro
The Remains of the Day

Ben Jonson
The Alchemist

James Joyce
Dubliners

John Keats
Selected Poems

Philip Larkin
High Windows
The Whitsun Weddings and Selected Poems

Christopher Marlowe
Doctor Faustus
Edward II

Ian McEwan
Atonement

Arthur Miller
All My Sons
Death of a Salesman

John Milton
Paradise Lost Books I & II

Toni Morrison
Beloved

George Orwell
Nineteen Eighty-Four

Sylvia Plath
Selected Poems

William Shakespeare
Antony and Cleopatra
As You Like It
Hamlet
Henry IV Part I
King Lear
Macbeth
Measure for Measure
The Merchant of Venice
A Midsummer Night's Dream
Much Ado About Nothing
Othello
Richard II
Richard III
Romeo and Juliet
The Taming of the Shrew
The Tempest
Twelfth Night
The Winter's Tale

Mary Shelley
Frankenstein

Richard Brinsley Sheridon
The School for Scandal

Bram Stoker
Dracula

Jonathan Swift
Gulliver's Travels and A Modest Proposal

Alfred Tennyson
Selected Poems

Alice Walker
The Color Purple

Oscar Wilde
The Importance of Being Earnest
A Woman of No Importance

Tennessee Williams
Cat on a Hot Tin Roof
The Glass Menagerie
A Streetcar Named Desire

Jeanette Winterson
Oranges Are Not the Only Fruit

John Webster
The Duchess of Malfi

Virginia Woolf
To the Lighthouse

William Wordsworth
The Prelude and Selected Poems

W. B. Yeats
Selected Poems